Living
in
Mao's Era
A Memoir

Jenton Johnson

authorHOUSE®

AuthorHouse™
1663 Liberty Drive
Bloomington, IN 47403
www.authorhouse.com
Phone: 1 (800) 839-8640

Published by AuthorHouse 09/24/2018

ISBN: 978-1-5462-6052-3 (sc)
ISBN: 978-1-5462-6051-6 (e)

Library of Congress Control Number: 2018911076

Print information available on the last page.

Any people depicted in stock imagery provided by Getty Images are models, and such images are being used for illustrative purposes only.
Certain stock imagery © Getty Images.

This book is printed on acid-free paper.

Because of the dynamic nature of the Internet, any web addresses or links contained in this book may have changed since publication and may no longer be valid. The views expressed in this work are solely those of the author and do not necessarily reflect the views of the publisher, and the publisher hereby disclaims any responsibility for them.

To my parents
Who set excellent examples to me.

Contents

Preface

Nearly all published memoirs are about eminent people, because their lives are extraordinary. This memoir is also about an extraordinary life: the life in Mao's era of 27 years. After the People's Republic of China was founded in 1949, the iron curtain was descended, as Winston Churchill put it. The life in Mao's era is pretty much opaque to the West.

It is true that some people have published books about their lives under Mao, such as "Life and Death in Shanghai" by *Nian Chen*, "Single Tear" by *Wu Ningkun*, "Wild Goose" by Jung Chang, "Son of Revolution" by *Liang Heng* and Judith Shapiro, "Sider Eater" by Rae *Yang*, and "Red Scarf Girl" by *Ji-li Jiang*. However, the authors of the first two books had finished their college education before the PRC was founded. The authors of the other books had not entered college when the Cultural Revolution started.

I am the generation who just entered elementary school when the PRC was founded. By the time the Cultural Revolution started in 1966, I was in my senior year in college. Those who entered college from 1961 – 1965 obtained a collective name: *Lao Wu Jie* (Old College Graduates of Five Years). Starting in 1966, no single college enrolled any student for five years or more, due to the Cultural Revolution. So, "old" was added in the collective name to indicate that these college graduates entered college before the Cultural Revolution.

Up to now, I have not seen the English memoir published by an author from the Old College Graduates of Five Years. So, there is a gap between the memoirs of the elder and younger generations. One possible reason to cause this gap is that the elder generation studied English in their foreign language class before the PRC was founded, and younger generations also studied English after China and the Soviet Union publicly broke up in the 1960s. When the PRC was founded, the Soviet Union was among the first foreign countries establishing diplomatic relationship with the PRC. In the 1950s, the Soviet Union was called the Big Brother. So, learning Russian could help us to follow the steps of the Soviet Union towards the communist society. The Ministry of Education of China decided that we should learn Russian in the foreign language class, rather than English. As a result, only a few of our generation who studied English later by themselves. The limited English abilities might have hindered our generation from writing their English memoirs.

It is also true that many history books have been written to account for Mao's era and the Cultural Revolution, but these books are more or less like the bird's eye view, and are focused more on big events, rather than the daily life of the ordinary people. Also, the vast majority of those books are based on secondary materials. In this book, I try to faithfully record the typical and real life of ordinary city dwellers during the Mao's era.

After the "reform and open-up" policy initiated by Deng Xiaoping, more and more westerners have gone to China for business, tours, and education. China has since achieved a great deal and becomes the second largest economy in the world. But the lives during the Mao's era are no longer there for visitors to see.

For all these reasons, I believe it is my obligation to tell the story of my generation in Mao's era. I started learning English after President Nixon visited China. This study eventually allowed me to pass the TOEFL and GRE to pursue my PhD degree in the United States. After retiring, I finally have more time and decided to write this memoir.

So many years have passed since Mao's death in 1976. Many institutions and universities have changed names or combined with some other institutions and universities. In this memoir, the old names of institutions and universities during Mao's era are used.

The Chinese Pinyin uses 26 Latin letters, but the pronunciations of these letters are different from the ones in English. To make it easier for English readers to read the names of the cities, provinces, mountains, rivers, etc., which are not well-known, I use the first letter, in capital, of the Pinyin, plus a hyphen, and plus word "city" or "river" etc. for their names, such as

L-city, G-river, etc. In case where the city names have the same first Pinyin letter, a second letter would be added, to distinguish them, such as Y-city and YK-city. Since the Pinyin is the guide to pronunciation, the capital letter and lower-case letter are equivalent. Sometimes I use the capital letter in Pinyin just for clarity. Many well-known Chinese figures, such as Deng Xiaoping, have been collected into the English dictionaries. However, some of them, such as Zhu De, are not familiar to some of the Chinese youngsters, let alone foreigners. Also, some places, such as Hankou that I think may not be widely known. In cases like these, I use Italian fonts, such as *Zhu De* and *Hankou*, in order to remind the reader that these are Chinese people or places.

To protect people's privacy, all the people's names in this memoir are false, except a few well-known public figures, such as Deng Xiaoping. Fortunately, the names of the people, places, and the schools are not essential to understand the story.

More details about the public events described in this memoir can be found from the Internet. The readers, who are interested in more details about the related event, photos, short videos, and movies of this era, can search the Internet. Many good history books that describe the big public events in Mao's era are also available.

Unlike many memoirs, which provide some related pictures. There is none in this memoir. As described in the chapter in the Army Farm, my home was burnt down due to a fire accident. My only album and other my belongings, which I did not bring with me, were also burnt. Cameras were luxury goods during Mao's era. The cheapest one, Sea Gull brand, cost three months of the starting salary of a college graduate. So, I did not own a camera and could not provide any relevant picture. Fortunately, there are a lot of pictures, movies, and videos from Mao's era on the Internet, which can supplement this memoir.

All quoted Mao's words, the related excerpts from the newspapers and documents, etc. were my English translation, not quoted from the officially published English versions, if any. Also, all the poems and the lyrics in this book are my own English translations. I have tried my best to truthfully translate them and believe that the key ideas of the original texts are conveyed in these translations.

I would like to use this opportunity to thank Dr. Stephen L. Rice, my PhD advisor, for reviewing the part of this memoir related to the Cultural Revolution (1966-1976), and providing extensive, detailed, and valuable feedback.

I would also like to thank the staff in AuthorHouse for their help, advice, and suggestions, especially Mary Abarquez, who spent a lot of time communicating with me during the publication process.

L-city (1943-1950)

My birth place L-city is on the bank of the upper stream of the Yellow River, and was a pivotal town along the ancient Silk Road. The Yellow River is actually clean in this section. The water becomes yellow after passing the yellow Loess Plateau, the flow flushes the soil into the river, and causes it to change color.

When I was born in 1943, we live in a house located in Z-road, and Daddy was the director of L-city office of the Alxa Trade Company, which was owned by the Mongolia prince *Dalizhaya*. Soon we moved to a new house near the W-mountain where my younger brother was born in 1946. About one year later, we moved again to a new house located in Y-road, where my younger sister was born in 1949. Since I was born, Mama stopped working and stayed home to take care of us kids.

This new house had two big yards, we lived in the front yard, and Mr. *Zhu*, Daddy's colleague and friend, and his family lived in the back yard. One day, I saw a middle-aged man, wearing sunglasses with a couple of servants, entered the yard and started calling Daddy. My brother and I looked at this stranger, wondering who he was. Daddy came out upon hearing the call and greeted him. Then he called us to greet the Mongolia prince *Dalizhaya*. From his clothes, I felt this Mongolia prince was just like a *Han*, who typically wore a jacket or shirt with a pant. The prince entered our house and had a lunch with us. He speaks fluent Mandarin, and was quite amiable.

L-city was not a big, densely populated metropolitan city at the time when I was born. There were only a couple of roads in the downtown area. The Yellow River Bridge, the landmark of L-city, was the first steel bridge across the Yellow River. I played there many times. A special river transportation tool used by the local people was the sheepskin raft. The raft consists of a dozen or more airtight whole sheep skins with the air blowing into each one. Then the balloon-like sheepskins are connected by a wood truss. When passengers were on the truss, most part of the sheepskins would sink down. This made the passengers looked like floating on the surface of the water. In the south part of the city was the W-mountain, with many Buddhist temples on the hillside. In the downtown of L-city, there was a small zoo with some tigers, bears, monkeys, etc. At the largest intersection in downtown, there was a church. Mama, a devout Christian, always brought us there on Sundays. We particularly liked going to the church on Christmas day because the Santa Clause in the church would give each child a bag of candy and toys as the Christmas gift.

There are many regional foods and snacks. Vendors frequently used carrying-poles or carts to travel around the streets and lanes to sell their goods. Those traveling vendors would make short melodious hawker's cries. The cries were different from each other. But the vendors who sold the same goods would make the same melodious cry.[1] So, by hearing these hawker's cries, people would know what vendors were nearby.

The most popular snack at that time was perhaps the roasted broad bean. The broad bean in L-city was about 50 percent larger than the ones in other areas. Roasted in the sands, the aroma of the broad bean always attracted me to the stall, and the broad bean becomes one of my lifelong favorite snacks. In winter, the temperature of this north-west city would be around 10°F, and the local people demonstrated their ingenuity by creating "hot D-pears," which is made by boiling D-pears, one of the juicy local pears, and adding buckwheat honey. When I heard the vendor's cry, I would run out to buy it.

There was also a juicy and sweet melon known as Wallace melon. In 1944 American Vice President Henry A. Wallace visited China, and brought some honeydew melon seeds as the gift to Chinese people. He wanted to help the people in north-west China to solve their problems caused by the very dry climate. The melon was successfully grown in L-city area and was named Wallace Mellon, because it was he who brought the seeds to China. After the Liberation[2], the name of Wallace melon was

---

[1] Since the late 1950s, those individual vendors disappeared. Now only some performers would imitate those melodious hawker's cries to tourists.

[2] Liberation is a common word used to mark the time the PRC was founded. After/before Liberation means after/before October 1, 1949.

changed to "*Bai Lan Gua*," which means white *Lan* melon, for its skin color is pale and grows in L-city area.[3]

In the summer of 1949, we had to flee L-city because the People's Liberation Army, or the PLA, marched toward the city and there would be a big battle. We managed to get on a truck and moved westward. Near sunset time, we arrived at a small town in the mountain area. The hotel was a row of caves, dug on a small hillside. A few days later, my sister and brother suffered from measles, one after the other. I had already had measles, so I was immune. Daddy was quite resourceful and had good knowledge and experience about Chinese herbal medicine. He managed to buy some herbs in the local herb store and cured both of them in a couple of days.

In one sunny morning, Mama brought us to the roadside to see Daddy off, because a messenger came and brought a letter from prince *Dalizhaya*, calling him and some other employees to go to the headquarter in B-town. We saw Daddy and about a dozen his colleagues in the trade company were on the horse backs. After saying goodbye, those men ran away to the northeast direction.[4] In the meantime, women and children with some service men continued their trip to the west. In the evening, we arrived at a village. We were arranged to live in a big courtyard compound. Inside the compound, there were a big yard and bungalows, which were built on the four sides. We saw only old men and women in the compound, and I was not able to find a kid to play with. A few days later, we heard some distant gun fires and explosions. But soon those sounds stopped. One afternoon, I saw a PLA soldier, with a rifle on his shoulder, walked in from the front door. He just inspected around the yard and walked away, without saying anything or disturbing anyone. A few days later, we heard that the battle was over and we could go home.

When back in L-city, we found our house and yard were intact. There was no sign of the battles in this neighborhood. We were told by neighbors that L-city had been liberated.

---

3   After the Liberation, the United States was regarded as the number one enemy of China. Therefore, it is improper to call a melon with an American name. In 1956 the melon's name was formally changed and used until present days.

4   Years later, Mother told me that Father was a member of the Prince *Dalizhaya*'s delegation to negotiate with the PLA, about peaceful liberation of Alxa area.

In the fall of 1949, Mama enrolled me in the elementary school near our home. This school used to be a Buddhist temple. After the Liberation, the religion was regarded as superstition and "spirit opium," which would be narcotic to people's thought. Priests and ministers of Churches were charged as the spies or the "running dogs"[5] of imperialists. As a result, most of the temples and churches were used either as government office buildings, schools, or dormitories of some government units. So, after the Liberation, Mama stopped going to the Church. Naturally, there had been no Christmas celebration since then.

We had two courses: Chinese and Arithmetic. Since Mama had taught me some Chinese characters and basic addition and subtraction, the classes were quite easy to me. One thing I can still remember is the physical punishment for students, who violated school rules. Once, all students were gathered to see the principal disciplining some students. When he was beating a student's palm with a ferule, I was scared. The physical punishment in schools was soon forbidden in China.

In the summer of 1950, our whole family left L-city to return to my parents' home province, J-province, where my grandparents, uncles and other relatives were living. We headed to *Xian* by a truck, because there was no railroad between L-city and *Xian* at that time. It took two days for us to travel the mountain road, and to arrive in *Xian*. We stayed in *Xijing* (Western Capital) Guest House for a few days. As an ancient capital, *Xian* is full of attractions. One of them is *Li Shan* (*Li* Mountain), where the famous hot spring *Huaqing* Spring was located. This hot spring had been for the royal families since the *Han* Dynasty (202 BC – 220 AD). Daddy brought us there, and we all enjoyed the natural warm water enormously.[6]

After the short stay, we continued our trip by train, and this was the first time I traveled by train. Unlike the automobile, the train moved so

---

[5]   The phrases about the dog reflected very different cultures between that of China and that of the West. All Chinese phrases associated with the dog are of negative connotations. Comparing the popular English saying: "The dog is man's best friend," with the well-known Chinese saying:" The dog would never change the habit of eating shit." In Chinese, the running dog, or "*zou gou*," means the accomplice.

[6]   The well-known Terracotta warriors, which Michelle Obama viewed in 2014, was not unearthed until 1974.

smoothly that I felt the train station moved backwards. On the train, there was a dining car, we went there for meals. I saw passengers drinking a dark Chocolate-colored liquid that I had never seen before. I asked Daddy what it was, he answered that it was "*ke kou ke le* (Coca Cola's Chinese translation)," which means "delicious and delightful" in Chinese. Upon hearing this attractive name, I was itching to try it, and was thrilled by its taste. Not until more than three decades later, did I drink it again in 1983. Because there was no diplomatic relationship between the People's Republic of China and the Unites States after the Liberation, Coca Cola disappeared from the mainland market shortly after this trip. In 1979 after China and the U.S. established diplomatic relationship, Coca Cola returned to the Chinese market again.

After two days, the train arrived at *Hankou*, which is located on the north bank of the Yangtze River, and is one of the three cities of *Wuhan*. We stayed there shortly to purchase ship tickets from *Hankou* to J-city, which is the city on the south bank of the Yangtze River, and located in north of J-province. In *Hankou*, Daddy managed to buy tickets to watch Beijing opera "The Sorcerer and the White Snake" played by Mr. *Mei Lanfang*,[7] who was famous for playing female characters, and was one the four best actors of Beijing Opera at that time. In this opera, *Mei Lanfang* played the heroine, and *Mei Baijiu*, his son, played her maid. I was amazed to know that the two major female characters in the opera were played not by two actresses but by two actors. Daddy was a big fan of *Mei Lanfang*. He was so enthusiastic that he went to the back stage to show his admiration, and to shake hands with Mr. *Mei* and his son, after the show.

We took ship for our next leg. It was also the first time we travel by ship. The ship was stable and quiet in comparison to the train, which would generate click-clunk sound while moving. At first I thought the ship was not moving at all. Only after a while did I notice that the scene outside the window became different. We spent a night and a day on the ship and arrived at J-city in the evening of the following day. After staying in a hotel for the night, we continued our trip by train on the next day. By noon, we arrived at our destination: N-city.

---

[7]   Mr. *Mei Lanfang* visited the United States in 1930s.

N-city (1950-1953)

We temporarily lived in a hotel. The first night when we were about to sleep, a loud siren sounded outside. When lived in L-city, I never heard such a siren sound. As it turned out, it was from the fire engines. We were told that there was a fire along the bank of the G-river. We could see the sky was lightened in dark red color by the flame. It took a couple of hours for the firefighters to put out the fire, and hundreds of homes were destroyed. This was the first time in my life to see such a disaster caused by fire.

N-city was a much more densely populated city than L-city, and the streets near our hotel were crowded. In addition, the public transportation system and other public facilities, such as parks, theaters, and hospitals were much more developed than that of L-city. I noticed that the bus in N-city had a big cylinder-shaped device on its back. I did not know what the device was used for. Daddy told me that these buses were burning water gas, because in that area gasoline was not as plentiful as in L-city. The big cylinder-shaped device at the rear side of the bus was a water gas generator. Charcoal and water were used to generate the "water gas" as the fuel.

After a quick visit to our grandparents in H-town, which is about 140 miles east of N-city, Daddy left N-city to continue working for the newly established the People's Government of B-town, headed by Mongolian prince *Dalizhaya*.

After Daddy left, Mama, my brother, sister, and I moved to a house located at 16 East Dragon Lane, and was owned by Mr. *Yang*, one of our relatives. His wife's younger sister was the wife of my younger uncle (my mother's younger brother), and his wife's younger brother married my third aunt, one of my mother's younger sisters.

The house was a two-story building with a small yard. On the first floor, there was a big dining room, two big bedrooms, and one smaller bedroom. My maternal grandmother lived in the smaller bedroom. My elder uncle's (my mother's elder brother) family, and our family lived in each of the big bedrooms. The *Yang*'s family lived upstairs. He had three sons and two daughters. His elder daughter had left home to join the PLA. The younger daughter was in her final years in the elementary school. The eldest son was married and not yet had any child. The other two sons, whose pet names were Big *Lu* and Small *Lu* were still attending elementary schools. His youngest son was one year my senior. So my brother and I quickly befriended with *Yang*'s three younger kids.

It was the first time I met with my maternal grandmother and the elder uncle's family. Grandma followed the old foot-binding tradition, and had very small feet. She and Mama were both devout Christians. Soon after the Liberation, they could not find a church in N-city, so Mama frequently read the Chinese version of the Holy Bible to Grandma at home. They would pray before each meal, and frequently quote some stories and sayings from the Bible to teach us about morality, life, and the world.

My elder uncle was a professor teaching Chinese literature in the N-city University. Before the Liberation, the Chinese universities were similar to that of the Western comprehensive universities. In the early 1950s, the People's Government adjusted the higher educational system, following the education system in the Soviet Union, where there were many institutes specialized in various industries and professions, such as engineering institutes, medical institutes, etc. As a result, my elder uncle was transferred to the newly established H-province Teacher's Institute in C-city. His family also moved to C-city with him in 1952.

During that time, my younger uncle and aunt paid a brief visit to us. He was a professor and working in Beijing. Mama said that this uncle had studied in the United States.

After the Liberation, in May Day and October 1, the National Day of the PRC, there would be mass parades which attracted a large crowd of onlookers. Generally, the flag team came first, followed by big portrait boards. At the beginning were the portraits of some foreigners with mustaches and beards that people were not familiar with. Later I learned that they were Marx, Engels, Lenin, and Stalin. Then came the portraits of Chairman Mao and General *Zhu De*.[8] I heard people in the crowd commented that there was a mole near the center of Chairman Mao's chin, and according to the ancient Chinese *Xiang Mian Shu*,[9] such a mole is called emperor mole. This was why he became our new emperor. Soon, people learned the new title for Mao – Chairman Mao – not Mao His Majesty.

The portraits procession was followed by the PLA military band, and then followed by soldiers with various weapons. After that, there were civilian processions from various organizations. Each person in the civilian processions held a small colored triangular paper flag, with some slogan on it. In each unit, there was a man who would lead people to shout slogans. When shouting, the leading man would lift his right fist, as if punching into the sky. The rest of his unit would follow him by repeating the same slogan and gesture. The slogan that I heard the most and could understand was "Long Live Chairman Mao!" I had never seen such a parade in L-city.

In the fall semester of 1950, Mama enrolled me into the N-city Second Elementary School. All students were organized into classes.[10] My class had about 40 students. Each class had a *ban zhu ren* (Teacher-in-Charge). This Teacher-in-Charge would be responsible for various aspects of the class. He or she was also responsible for writing student reviews for each semester. For the new school year, in addition to Chinese and Arithmetic courses, three more courses were added: music, arts, and physical education. In the music class, we learned the national anthem and the song "The East is Red," which was the mostly hearing and singing song during the Mao's era. The first section of the lyrics was as follows:

"The east is red.
The sun is rising.

---

[8] Zhu De was the top leader of the red army in the red base in *Jinggang* Mountain in late 1920s. His name was often mentioned together with Mao, especially before the Liberation.

[9] The Chinese physiognomy which tells one's fortune by the facial features.

[10] In China, all schools, from the elementary school to the college, the students are organized into classes, each class has 30 – 50 students.

In China Mao Zedong comes.
He works for people's happiness.
Oh
Our great savior, he is!"

Around that time, the central government issued a regulation that the city dwellers were not allowed to keep dogs, because dogs were the major source of rabies, and dogs also competed for food with people. A campaign to eliminate dogs started. Dog owners had to turn in their dogs to the collection stations before a certain deadline. There were also many groups walking around streets to catch the straying dogs. In just a couple of months, the dog disappeared in N-city.

One day in October, we had an all-hands meeting. In the meeting, the school principal told us that American imperialist together with its follower Syngman Rhee crossed over the 38th parallel and invaded North Korea.[11] Now the aggressors approached the Yalu River and started bombarding some boarder cities of China. We were shown a lot of photos where the houses were said to be destroyed, and the people killed by American bombs. In the meantime, demonstrations by factories, institutions, and schools were organized to protest American aggressors and its followers. A political campaign called "*Kang Mei Yuan Chao; Bao Jia Wei Guo*[12] (Resist the American, help North Korean, and Protect our family and Homeland)" started. The Chinese volunteer army had crossed the Yalu River to fight in North Korea side by side with the brotherly North Korean Army.

There was also a political fund-raising campaign: "donation for fighter jets and cannons." It was said that the Chinese volunteer army was badly in need for more ammunitions and fighter jets. We students were mobilized to take part in the campaign. First, we were assigned the task of creating slide shows, based on the famous cartoon book "Adventures of *Sanmao*"

---

[11] Not until 1985 when I was in the University of Central Florida, did I know the truth about the Korean War. It was when I chatted in with Kim, a South Korean graduate student, about the Korea War in the school library. I told him what I heard since in the elementary school and he objected: "No! No! No!" Then he went to the history shelves to select a couple of books for me to read.

[12] "*Kang Mei Yuan Chao*" was the name of the Korea War in China. The phrase appeared in many news reports, novels, and movies, etc.

authored by *Zhang Leping*. We were given pieces of glass of 3 by 5 inches, with one side painted with white paint. Each of us was to make one slide by first tracing one page from the palm-sized pictorial book, and then using some sharp tool to remove the paint under the traced lines, and then to copy the short caption from the book. The light from the slide projector would go through the lines and the descriptions to form the pictures and captions on the screen. After we finished our slides, we submitted them to our Teacher-in-Charge. In the evenings, we would go out and show the story to the public. Every 20-30 minutes, the teacher would ask us to stop the show, and use the turntable to play a vinyl of the newly created song for "Resist the American, help North Korean, and Protect our family and Homeland" campaign. Here are its lyrics:

> "Valiantly and high-spiritedly,
> We cross the Yalu River.
> To defend peace and our homeland,
> Also to protect our families.
> Good sons and daughters of China,
> United into a single force.
> Resist the USA and help the North Korea,
> Defeat American wolves!"

In the meantime, we would use a small bamboo basket to collect the money donated by the onlookers. The money was then submitted to the school office, and in turn, to the city government, and finally to the central government.

In addition, we were organized to write letters of gratitude to uncles of the Volunteer Army soldiers, who were away from home to fight the war. With suggestions and sample letters from our teachers, we would write some short letters addressed to "Dear Uncles of the Volunteer Army" saying that we all appreciated their brave services in fighting American aggressors. Our letters were collected by our school, and then sent to the Chinese Volunteer Army in North Korea.

The political, or ideological education was an important part of our curriculum. We had political lectures to learn the basics of the People's

Republic of China. Some important points, repeatedly emphasized during the 1950s, were that in new China it was the people that were the master of the country, and that the government in new China was the "*Ren Min Zheng Fu* (People's Government)," which was entirely different from the previous government. The poster "Serve the People" in Chairman Mao's calligraphy is in every government building, inside, or outside, or both.

The political teacher also explained about the policies and the international situations, such as the Korean War, and the relationship with the "Big Brother," i.e. the Soviet Union. "The Soviet Union's today is our tomorrow" was a popular slogan at that time. We were organized to watch the free translated Soviet movies, which showed the happy life of the Soviet people. The farmers in collective farms used machines to plow land and harvest crops. They were smiling and singing songs while working in the field. To most Chinese, the life of the Soviet people in the movies was indeed like in paradise. As a result, learning from our Soviet brother was quite convincing. People were looking forward to our "tomorrow" so we could lead the same happy communist life as the Soviet people.

In addition to participate the above activities, we were also organized to attend some class struggle exhibitions. One such exhibition was in the old Y-park[13] near our school. It was about the campaign of the land reform. There were many paintings to describe how the Landlord cruelly exploited the Poor and Middle-Lower peasants. There were also jewelries, gold bars, luxurious clothes and furniture, confiscated from the families of the Landlords and Rich peasants. Their lands and houses were also confiscated and distributed to the Poor and Middle-Lower peasants. There were even photos shown the public executions of Landlords and counter-revolutionists. After the denouncing rallies, they were brought to the field and executed by the PLA soldiers, with hundreds of onlookers. This was the first time in my life to see the pictures of executed people. The grisly scenes terrified me.

At that time, there were large amounts of cloth printed with big flowers, imported from the Soviet Union. People called them "Russian Flowered Cloth." Some fashion-sensitive girls and ladies started to buy such cloth to make clothes, skirts, and "*bulaji.*"[14]

---

13   This park was changed into resident and commercial buildings several years later.

14   A one-piece Russian style dress-skirt combination for females.

But the quantity of the Russian cloth was so large that females alone could not consume them all. At that time, the males were accustomed to wearing single colored shirts, mainly the white shirt. If a man was wearing a flowered shirt, he would be laughed at for mistakenly wearing his wife's or sisters' clothes. Even boys refused to wear the flowered shirt fearing to be teased as "pseudo-girls." Nevertheless, the Party had its way. Through the New Democratic Youth League,[15] the official organization for youth, some young men were persuaded to throw away the outdated tradition, and to wear flowered clothes like the Soviet brothers.

One day, our young music teacher came wearing a shirt made of such a flowered cloth. Upon entering the classroom, we all laughed. The teacher was prepared and said with a sweet smile:

"Looks good, isn't it?" pointing to his shirt.

We all laughed more. Then he continued:

"Why don't you all wear the beautiful flowered shirt like me?"

Later, I did see more young men in the street wearing shirts made of the Soviet flowered cloth.

After the fund-raising for fighter jets and cannons, another political campaign, "Three antis" started in late 1951. The campaign related propaganda posters and cartoons were everywhere. Shortly after that, another campaign "Five Antis" started in early 1952. To us kids, we did not even recognize some characters used in those posters, let alone understood their meaning. So, we were not required to participate in those campaigns.

However, the political situation became more and more serious with time. One day when I was back from the school, I was told that *Yang's* eldest son, who was in his late 20s, was arrested because he once joined the "Three Democratic Youth League," the youth organization established by the KMT (*Guo Ming Tang*, or the Nationalist Party[16]). Joining any organization established by the KMT was regarded as counter-revolutionary, a serious political crime. A few days later, his young wife attempted to commit a suicide by swallowing a bottle of sleeping pills. When her attempt was discovered, she was quickly moved to a bamboo

---

[15]   It was late change to the Communist Youth League.

[16]   The National Party, or KMT, ruled China before the Liberation, and is one of the big parties in Taiwan.

chair, and carried to a nearest hospital. We children helped to carry her small personal items, and went with them. She survived this time, but killed herself in her second attempt by cutting her wrist in the hospital.

A couple of months later, Mr. *Yang* himself was arrested, and was transferred to a war criminal prison in *Shenyang*, the capital city of *Liaoning* province. Although he never worked in the military, he was a government legislator when the KMT was in power, therefore, he was regarded as a war criminal.

My third uncle, the husband of my third aunt, was a professor in the J-province Agricultural University in L-town, a small town about 15 miles south of N-city. At that time, my third aunt was a teacher working in Y-town, a small town in east of J-province. So, in Sundays, my third uncle would come to N-city and spent the weekend with his elder sister and brother-in-law's family. Every Saturday afternoon, I would go with small *Lu* to meet him at the bus station.

One Saturday, we waited several buses and did not see him. Seeing the sky was getting dark, and fearing our parents might be worrying about us, we reluctantly gave up and returned home. Returning home, we were stunned by the news that the third uncle had hanged himself.

He studied agriculture in Japan and returned to China in response to the call for all oversea Chinese intellectuals to return to build the new China. But shortly after he returned, the campaign of "Thought Reformation for Intellectuals" started. During the campaign, like all the returned oversea intellectuals, my third uncle was asked repeatedly to expose his bourgeois thoughts deep inside his head, and to do self-criticism. Nobody could pass it in the first few rounds of the self-criticism because it was invariably regarded as not deep enough. Unable to bear the pressure, he ended his young life. To us kids, he was optimistic, humorous, elegant, and knowledgeable. He was also an excellent story teller, who always attracted us when talking. We could hardly imagine how such a sunny person would kill himself.

Next day, my third aunt came to N-city with her newborn boy, upon receiving the telegram sent to her. During her stay in N-city for the funeral, I often heard her long sobbing at night from upstairs. While sobbing, she also murmured, as if talking to her beloved husband who could no longer hear her. Her sobs were light and soft, but heartbroken.

Mr. *Yang's* second daughter was the oldest among us. In the summer of 1952, she graduated from the elementary school, and was admitted to a teacher's school. After three years of study, the graduate from the teacher's school would teach in elementary schools.

She liked books, and had read many Chinese novels as well as translations of Russian books. Influenced by her, we all loved books, and frequently visited the *Xinhua* Bookstore run by the government[17]. One day, we went there, and I found an interesting text only book, rather than the children's pictorial books with text captions. I was so absorbed by the story that I totally forgot about the time, until they called me to go home for dinner. This was a milestone in my life, and from then on I became a lifelong book lover.

On March 5, 1953, there was a breaking news that Stalin died of a stroke. The principal of our school announced it with tears. He said Stalin was our great benefactor and friend. Under his leadership, the Soviet Union gave us innumerable help and support. His death was the great loss not only for the Soviet people, but for Chinese as well. He then recommended that we buy the portrait of Stalin and hang on the wall with a black silk belt around it, to make a personal memorial. He also recommended that we buy black armbands to wear as a way of mourning. This was what we did.

Finally, at the start of the state funeral in Moscow, all factories, trains, boats and ships in China would whistle for three minutes. Hearing this sound, everyone should stand still in silence to honor Stalin.

In summer of 1953, after our semester ended, we left N-city to join Daddy in B-town, a small town, west of the H-mountain, in the northwest of China.

---

[17]   During Mao's time, there was only one book store chain with the name "*Xinhua* Bookstore."

B-city (1953-1958)

At that time, there was no railroad led to B-town. We had to travel in two legs. First, we took train from N-city to *Xian*. Then we would travel by cars.

When we arrived at the guest house in *Xian*, a jeep had been there waiting for us, and the driver, Mr. Wang, prince *Dalizhaya's* chauffeur, received us warmly. Next day, we set out to B-town, and several other people were coming with us. A truck carried the other people and our luggage. It took two days for us to reach Y-city, the capital city of N-autonomous region. We stayed there overnight and continued our trip on the following day. By noon, we arrived at a small station in a rest area, located in a small pass on the H-mountain. To us this station looked like ancient castle, with an old gatekeeper working there. This made the scene like a movie setting.

After lunch, we were on the road again, and in the late afternoon, we arrived at B-town. There was a brick town-wall enclosing this old town. We went in through two gates on the south wall near the southwest corner. The two gates were arranged in such way that the outer gate was facing the east, and the inter gate facing the south. The advantage of this right-angle arrangement was that in case the enemy broke the outer gate, this angled arrangement and the small maneuver area would make the enemy harder to enter the inner gate. The gate was built in the Qing dynasty with its name in Chinese characters engraved above the outer gate.

Entering the two gates, our jeep made a right turn and stopped at the front gate of the Palace of Mongolian Prince *Dalizhaya*. The front gate had two stone lions, like the ones in many old mansions in Beijing. It was said that this small town was built to imitate the Forbidden City. For this reason, B-town is called little Beijing in the desert. As many old buildings in Beijing, the palace's main gate faced south.

Pointing at a middle-aged man with gray hairs standing by the jeep, Mama said to me: "Have you greeted your Daddy?" Seeing his gray hairs, I was not sure he was Daddy. Three years ago, his hairs had been totally black and looked much younger. After some hesitation, I greeted Daddy, and he smiled. Only years later, when recalling the suicide of my third uncle, did I realize what kind of stress Daddy had gone through, during these political campaigns. That might be a major factor to cause his hair to grow gray.

We followed him entering the front gate, and saw a big courtyard. In the yard, we made a right turn, going through a short passageway, and entered a smaller courtyard. Our house was right on the east side of the yard. There was no electricity at that time. We had to use candles or kerosene lamps. Going to bed, I held a candle and walked into the bedroom and put the candle on one windowsill. The window was made of a latticed wood frame and covered with white translucent paper. Some air flow caused the candle flame to veer towards the window, the paper was on fire immediately. I was scared, and did not know what to do. Seeing the light of the flame, Mama rushed in, using her bamboo fan in hand to beat the flame, and was able to put out the fire quickly. This first night fire turned out to be a bad omen for us.

There were more than a dozen families lived in the palace in addition to the prince's family. Prince *Dalizhaya* lived on the northeast corner. It was a big yard with a western style one story building, and painted with light yellow color.

One day when I was playing with other kids in his yard, I heard somebody calling me. I saw an amiable mid-aged man standing in front of the yellow building and waving at me. Going closer, I still could not recognize him. So I asked him how he would know my name. He smiled brightly, and said:

"I would not tell you. Go and ask your father about it."

As it turned out, he was Prince *Dalizhaya*! He had seen me when we lived in L-city, but I forgot this encounter.

He had seven children. Except the sixth child, all other were girls. His son, the sixth child, was about my age, and was one of my classmates.

The youngest girl was about my younger brother's age, and they were classmates.

A small oasis, B-town's east is the H-mountain and west is Tengger Desert. A few days after we arrived, my brother and I decided to explore the town wall. A town or city wall was for defense and security purpose, and would have four sides with a gate at the center of each side. Due to the local terrain, only the east and the south sides of the town wall had gates. The town wall was built along the hills, looking just like the Great Wall.

Our adventure started by climbing the east gate and going counter-clockwise. We discovered that in the middle of the north side, there was a small temple of *Guan*. Mr. *Guan* was a general during the Three Kingdom era (220 – 280 A.D.), and became the sworn-brothers with other two from different areas. General *Guan's* character embodied all the virtues highly valued in the Chinese culture, such as strong loyalty to his sworn-brothers, never forgot those who once treated him well, etc. So, after his death, he was regarded as a god and worshiped.[18]

The town wall divided the city into two parts: the inner and the outer. The inner town was about 0.5 square miles, and the outside is much larger stretching mainly in the east, the south, and the west directions, because there was a small mountain on the north, which prevented it from expanding in that direction. The inner city had many buildings used to be the palaces of princes, including Prince *Dalizhaya's* palace. After the Liberation, some of the palaces were used as the government office buildings, until the new office compound was built around 1956 in the far west of the city. There were other residential houses, general stores, bakery shops, tailor shops, an elementary school, and the local PLA garrison.

There was a large Lamaism temple, the Y-temple, next to the back door of *Dalizhaya's* Palace. In front of the temple, there was a small square about 50 yard by 50 yard. The temple's south-facing main gate was shut most of the time. There were two smaller doors on each side. The small door in the west opened more frequently, and sometimes we would see Lamas walking in and out through that door. Once when the door was open, my

---

[18]   *Guan* temples are everywhere in the mainland as well as in Taiwan, Hong Kong and some other places.

brother and I peered inside. There were quite a few big buildings behind the main gate, as well as rows of trees.

On the 15th of the January in Lunar calendar, there would be a big ritual show in the front square of this temple. The lamas from the temple would wear colorful costumes to play various religious figures in Lamaism. These figures would dance one by one around the square accompanied by percussion instruments. A couple of very long tube-shaped instruments, which could produce a loud bass sound, would be played from time to create special effects. There would be a figure wearing a human skeleton costume, representing the evil. Among the positive force was a figure wearing a deer head mask. Near the end of the show, a stand, like a miniature of the high-jump stand, was set up in the center of the square. The dear figure would dance around a couple of times, stop near the stand, and then use his antler to remove the horizontal stick. At that moment, the evil would fall down. This would indicate that the positive force had defeated the evil force, and people would be blessed in the coming New Year.

One day, my brother and I saw a very young lama walking out of the small side door of the temple. We waved to him. He smiled, and walked toward us. While we were wondering whether this little Mongolian was able to speak Chinese, he started talking to us in fluent Chinese, in local dialect, just like Han kids. He was about the same age as my younger brother, so we quickly became friends. We often met in the front square and played together. He told us many interesting stories about Buddhism, Lamaism, about their life in the temple, as well as the names of various Buddhas. He named many Buddhas' names that we never heard of. But finally he mentioned a name we had been very familiar with: "Chairman Mao is our greatest Buddha!"

Several days later, the little lama brought us some necklaces made of red threads, with a knot. He told us that there was a Buddha inside the knot. Some of the better necklaces had a small button with a tiny Buddha painted on it. Wearing this Buddha necklace, evils and ghosts would not dare to get close, so we would be safe, he told us. With limited allowance at that time, both my brother and I could only afford the cheapest knotted necklace. When putting them to our necks, he also performed some ritual and chanted something we could not understand. Then he told us that we were protected.

One night, when we went to sleep, Mama noticed our red necklaces. She asked us what they were. We told her everything about the little lama. Mama said that we were Christians and protected by Jesus Christ. So we do not need the necklaces. So, we took them off.

Mama liked to raise chickens. One day, our hen started hatching eggs. With great interest, we observed the process and watched the chicks growing. At first, we saw the hen would call the chicks to eat whenever she found some food and broke it into small pieces.

The hen was also extremely protective of her chicks. One day, a dog ran by, the hen was so brave as to fly toward the dog, and to peck him. The dog escaped quickly.

However, some weeks later, I noticed the hen no longer share her food with her children. Whenever the hen found some food and the chicks tried to come and eat as before, the hen would peck them away. I was puzzled as to why the hen no longer recognized her children. I asked Mama. She told me that it was not because that the mother no longer recognized her children, but because the hen wanted to force the chicks to learn to find food by themselves. Without this skill, the chicks would starve to die when the hen mother dies. I was amazed by the wonder of the nature.

Outside the south gates there was a big open area with a large and old elm tree. The local people called the open area "Under-the-Big-Tree," which was a major area for the local people to gather for chatting, playing poker, Chinese Chess, and taking sunshine along the south town wall during the winter.

There were many small vendors selling local snacks, fruits, and various special foods. On the west side of the town wall, there were several small blacksmith shops, where the workers were making kitchen knives, household items, and farming tools. The hammer pounding sounds gave this small remote town vivid living signs.

Outside the east gate, there was a road leading to a lake, or Lao Ba, by the local dialect. There were a lot of reeds along the edge of this lake. Near the lake, there was a big spring. An open channel led the water westwards toward the town. The channel provided the resident with the drinking water.

Local farmers lived in the outer area. Farm lands were mainly on the east and the south parts. They mainly grew wheats, corns, millets, and various vegetables. There was a plenty of fruits during the summer and fall, such as the various melons, peaches, apricots, apples, and Sha Zao, or "Sandy jujube," a local specific kind of fruit, which looks like a small jujube. Inside the skin, the pulp looks sandy. This is why it gets this name.

In winter, some vendors would put a stove on the side of the street, boiling chopped sheep offal with the powder of the red hot-pepper. In cold winter, the temperature often around ten-degree Fahrenheit, the aroma of the soup would certainly attract people. Indeed, after eating a bowl of such a delicious sheep offal soup, one would certainly feel warm.

From time to time, some traders from other places would come to Under-the-Big-Tree selling traditional herbal medicines, soaps, and other basic commodities. Those traders normally knew some magic tricks, and performed them to attract people. When the crowd became large enough, they would start selling. At early 1950s, there was no dentist office or dentist department in the local hospital. Sometimes, travelling dentists would come, and their main operation was to extract bad teeth. Later, when a new hospital was built, I no longer saw those travelling dentists.

Sometimes there were livestock fairs for individuals to buy, sell, or exchange sheep, horses, camels, mules, and donkeys. A broker would serve as a middle man. Unlike oral bargaining in most businesses, during the fair, people negotiate silently in a special way by connecting sleeves and using fingers to indicate prices inside the connected sleeves. When a seller and a buyer wanted to trade, they would negotiate prices through a broker. The buyer would offer a price first through the connected sleeves. Then the broker would tell the seller the offer price in the same way. The seller might make a counter offer, and the broker would pass it to the buyer. The bargaining might come back and forth for several times. If the buyer and seller finally agreed, they would leave the market to settle the deal. Otherwise, they would continue looking for other opportunities. But such folk fairs disappeared around the middle of the 1950s.

Starting from Under-the-Big-Tree, there was a street along the north -- south direction. It was about one mile long with the bridges over the three streams. The streams were usually small and the water was clean. Occasionally, when there was a thunder storm in the H-mountain area, the streams could be flooded with muddy water. On both sides of this street, there were shops, restaurants, doctors' offices, two movie theaters, and a cultural center, where there was a public library, and some rooms for playing Ping Pong, poker, etc. This was a major commercial street in the town.

At that time, this small remote town had no modern pollutions by noises, lights, and other industrial emissions. The air was so clean that the stars and the Milky Way were very clear at night. Also, the town was so quiet that we could frequently hear folk songs from afar by Mongolian herdsmen. There was no public transportation. People mainly shuffled along on foot, which were jokingly dubbed "Bus 11," because the two legs were similar to the number 11.

After developing my reading habit in N-city, the first thing I did shortly after we arrived here was to visit the public library. It was very small and had one librarian. All books were stored in one room. I applied for a library card and started borrowing books. Soon my younger brother also applied for a card, and borrowed books as well. But before long, we have read all the children's books available in this small library. Fortunately, a new *Xinhua* Bookstore opened. It was twice as far as the public library. But we still visited the book store frequently. At that time, the shelves were open to the buyers.[19] We could freely select books to read in the store.

In this area, the major energy source was coal, which was produced in the H-mountain area. The coal seller would use camels to carry coal from the mines to nearby towns and villages. There was a bell hang on the neck of the last camel of the caravan. When people heard the bell and needed to buy coal, they would come out and call the seller. In the winter, especially in the snowy days, Daddy would give more money to sellers than they would ask. I asked why. He said that the snowy and icy roads were extremely hard to walk. They were not easy, and deserved more for their goods.

---

[19] Some years later, book shelves were separated by a counter so that the buyer had to ask the salesperson to take the book. But the bookshelves were re-open again several years after the Cultural Revolution ended.

During the first few years after we arrived, the government office building was in a prince's palace, next to the *Dalizhaya's*. Daddy worked in the department of transportation for the local People's Government. He made many Mongolian friends there, and they often dropped in for a chat. They all could speak Mandarin fluently. Unlike most *Han* men, who smoked cigarettes, Mongolian men liked snuff. When Daddy smoked cigarettes, the Mongolian guests would take out their delicate snuff-bottles, and take pinches of snuff. Seeing they enjoyed snuff so much, I asked to try it. Upon snuffing, I sneezed immediately. All of the guests and Daddy broke into roaring laughter.

At noon, a serviceman in the government building would use a small, short tube device to make a very loud explosion sound. I asked Daddy, what this was. He told me that it was *Wupao* or Noon-Time-Gun, announcing that it was 12 o'clock sharp. At that time, clocks and watches were very expensive. An alarm clock cost at least 20 *Yuan ren min bi* (people's currency), or *RMB*[20] *for short, and a wrist watch cost more than 100 Yuan RMB* or more. Owning them was regarded as a luxury, because the local people's average monthly income was about 20 *Yuan* RMB. So, most residents in the town did not have a clock, and this *Wupao* sound could help people with the time.

In Mao's era, there were six working days a week.[21] In Saturday evening, the government compound would have a weekend dance party. Daddy frequently went there, and brought us with him. There were about 30 workers in the party, and two *Er-Hu*[22] and an accordion accompanying the dancers. All government workers wore gray *Zhong Shan* suit,[23] now known as the Mao suit in the West. Female government workers favored the Lenin Suit, which came from the Soviet Union, and was very similar to the double-breasted lady's suit.

In early September 1953, Mama brought me to the Second Elementary School and enrolled me in the fourth grade. The school was close to the

---

[20]   In1955, the government issued the second set of RMB, with old 100 *yuan* = new 1 cent. The currency in this book is based on this 1955 bill.

[21]   China started five working days a week on May 1, 1995.

[22]   A two-string Chinese music instrument.

[23]   The suit was designed by Dr. *Sun Zhong-Shan*, or Dr. Sun Yat-sen.

western town wall and the part of it was used as the school's wall. Rows of bungalows were classrooms and administrative offices. There was a basketball court, some simple wood parallel bars and horizontal bars for students to play.

For the fourth grade, we had Arithmetic, Abacus, Chinese, Physical Education, Music, and Art classes. To make sure we would go to school on time, Daddy bought a luxury item: an alarm clock, with two bells on the top. We were required to attend school at 7:00 am for a 45 minute self-study session. The formal class started at 8:00 am.

Since Beijing time was used nationwide in China, in winter, it was still quite dark at 7:00 am in B-town. Without electricity at that time, students had to bring kerosene lamps for the self-study session. Everyone used a kerosene lamp made of an empty ink bottle. By drilling a hole in the bottle's cover, and putting a section of cotton thread through the hole, a poor man's kerosene lamp was produced. Putting it on the small student's desk, we had adequate light for reading and writing. When it became light, we could see our nostrils were darkened by the smoke of the lamps.

One year later, we had electricity in the evening and early morning. Those self-made kerosene lamps were no longer needed. It was said at that time that "electric lights and telephones upstairs and downstairs" was the key feature of the communist paradise. Well, with the electric lights available, we were half way to that heavenly paradise. We were told that in the communist society, we would "do whatever we can, and take whatever we need."

Mr. *Wu*, our arithmetic and abacus teacher, was from *Shandong* province. His *Shandong* dialect was not hard to understand. With years of experience, he created some short poems for the rules to perform the abacus and the arithmetic calculation involving addition, subtraction, multiplication and division. After remembering those poems, most of us were able to perform those calculations with ease.

Another main class was Chinese, which involved reading, composition, and calligraphy. Mr. *Li*, our teacher of Chinese literature, was from *Henan* province. Like Mr. *Wu*, he also spoke his home dialect, rather than Mandarin. But unlike Mr. *Wu, who* always looked serious, Mr. *Li* smiled all the time. I liked the way he read some poems using his *Henan* dialect, and felt the poems sounded especially beautiful this way. I was one of his favorite students. Many times, he praised my compositions and read them to the whole class. This made me enjoy his literature class very much.

He was a fan of Mr. *Lu Xun*, one of the famous Chinese writers in the 1920s. In addition to the regular lessons, he frequently used the last few minutes of his class to read some excerpts from Mr. *Lu*'s books. As a result, we all became the fans of Mr. *Lu Xun*.

In our literature textbook, in addition to the regular lessons, there were many heroic stories about the Chinese Volunteer Army. For example, Mr. *Huang Jiguang* who used his body to block the machine gun of a fort, so that his comrades could charge ahead; Airforce hero Mr. *Zhang Jihui* who shot down the elite American pilot Davis, etc.

June 1 is the Children's Day in China. June 1, 1954 was the first Children's Day in my life. Each of us was given a small bag of candies, peanuts, and cookies. We were taught the Song of the Children's Day:

> "Flowers are blooming in June,
> And the sun is lovely.
> June 1 is the Children's Day,
> Happy songs are all over the places.
> We sing for our happiness,
> We sing for our prosperous motherland.
> With international children,
> Together we sing joyfully.
> Our languages are different,
> But the same song we are all singing:
> Peace, peace, peace,
> The common wish of the mankind!"[24]

In summer vacations, Daddy started to introduce some classical Chinese poems, proses, and novels to us. He first asked us to learn some short *Tang* Dynasty poems by heart, and then asked us to learn some good classical prose poems by heart. He told us not to worry about some phrases or sentences that we could not fully understand.

"You will understand more when you go over them each time," he said.

---

[24] This was the original lyrics I learned. Late, it was modified multiple times to become more and more communistic.

He was a good story teller. Upon our request, he would tell us the stories from the most famous classical novels. This greatly whetted our interest in the classical literature, as well as history.

New school year started in September 1954, and I entered the fifth grade. My younger brother also enrolled in the first grade. He was a very diligent student and made straight A in his classes. He late kept this record for all his school years.

In the fifth grade, three more classes were added: history, geography, and science. I loved those new classes because they were really eye-opening. The geography teacher frequently asked us to find important mountains, rivers, and cities on the map. All students were in the competition to find the names on the map as quickly as possible. The student who was the first to find the name would be praised and invited to point it out on the big map hanging on the blackboard.

The science teacher would spend a half of his class answering whatever questions we would have. The most amazing lesson was when the teacher told us the human being was evolved from apes. Upon hearing this, we were all surprised in disbelief:

"Why do we still see various monkeys and apes?"
"Why didn't all monkeys become human?"
…

The teacher explained that the evolution took an extremely long time, the changes were so subtle that we would not detect them in our lifetime. Nevertheless, most of us were not fully convinced during the class.

One day, there was a solar eclipse in the morning. Our science teacher organized us to observe. He gave each of us a piece of 3X5 sized glass, darkened by the smoke from a kerosene lamp, and then observe the sun through this darkened glass. We were all amazed to see that part of the sun became dark and the size of the dark part changed with time until the sun became round again.

In1954, the central government issued "the General Lines of Policy in Transition Period," which was the guidelines for the country to transit from New Democratic society to Marx-Leninism Socialist society. In order to convey the spirit of this general line, students were mobilized for the propaganda work. Students in fifth and sixth grades, or in senior elementary grades, were relatively well-educated compared to the majority of the local farmers, who were either illiterate or with very little education.

We were given some condensed and simplified materials to study, and our teachers would explain some difficult parts in lectures. The key idea was to persuade the farmers to actively respond to the call by the government to join the Agricultural Cooperative.

After the preparation, we were divided into small groups of 3 or 4 students and visit the homes of farmers. We were too young to understand many of the political jargons used in the materials, so we just read the propaganda materials to those farmers. They showed great respect to us, listened quietly, and did not raise any question, until we finished. After the propaganda session, the whole family would courteously see us off in front of their houses, treated us like the government cadre. This made us quite proud of ourselves.

After this experience, some of my classmates were excited and wanted to make more propaganda by creating a wall newspaper. Mr. *Yu*, one of my classmates, and I discussed this idea with our younger brothers. Upon hearing our proposal, the two youngsters eagerly joined us. We had a meeting and discussed the details. After reviewing some newspapers, we thought that the potential readers would be local farmers. Therefore, the pictorial would be a better choice.

We collected pictures from various sources and copied them into smaller paper pads, and then pasted them into a big paperboard with the title in big characters: "Wall Newspaper, First Issue." Under the title, we put smaller characters: "Edited by Four Students from the Second Elementary School." Out of shyness, we waited until it was dark to post it when there was nearly nobody in the street.

But quickly our classmates found out who had published it. Some started to attack us by asking who had given us the permission to use the name of the Second Elementary School in our wall newspaper. Facing the group of attackers, I was in a panic and did not know what to say. But Mr. *Yu* countered calmly:

"Didn't you guys see the editors are four students from the Second Elementary School? Are we not the students of this school?"

This made those attackers fall into silence. With a breath of relief, I admired his quick wit.

Nevertheless, those students reported this event to the leaders of our school, and we were called to the principal's office. The principal told us that publishing was not a children's play, and that we should have consulted our teachers or school leaders before anything went public, because any mistake in the politic issues would have serious consequences. After that, our enthusiasm and interest in the publication were like a basketball with a hole punched on it, and never did this again.

In 1955, learning from the Soviet Union, the school started to set up the Young Pioneer organization. Those, who made a good grade in the study and obeyed the school's rules, were admitted. Like wearing a tie, the member would wear a triangular red scarf, which represents a corner of a red flag. The way of saluting by the Young Pioneer member was to lift right hand above the head, with the open palm facing the front. We were told that this gesture means the people's interest was above all.

Soon, most students, including my brother and me, became the Young Pioneer members and wore red scarfs. We were taught the Song of the Young Pioneer. Its lyrics were written by the famous poet Mr. *Guo Moruo*, and the music composed by Mr. *Ma Sicong*[25], the president of the Central Conservatory of Music at that time. The first section of the lyrics was:

> "We are the children of the New China,
> We are Young Pioneers.
> United to succeed our revolutionary predecessors,
> Fear no difficulties nor the heavy duties.
> Strive to build New China,
> Follow the Great Leader Mao Zedong!"[26]

---

[25] He was persecuted during the Cultural Revolution and managed to escape to Hong Kong and then to the U.S.

[26] This song was replaced in 1978 by "We are Communist Successors," the theme song of the movie "Little Heroic Eighth Army."

In 1956, B-town set up a wired broadcasting station. A speaker box was provided for each subscriber's family. It was wired to the city's broadcast station. The broadcast started in the evening, mainly to replay the radio programs from the China National Radio, especially the half an hour "News and Newspaper Abstracts program," which frequently broadcasted the important editorials of the People's Daily and announced key messages from the Central Government.

In addition, some children-oriented newspaper and magazines were published, such as "Chinese Youngster's Newspaper," which used simpler language to explain the Party's history and policies. Among the revolutionary stories was the Long March. The red army soldiers had to eat leather belt and grass roots during the difficult time.

Near the end of the spring semester, most of the students in the school took the entrance examination for entering middle school. I did well in my exam, and was admitted to the First Middle School of B-town.

In the summer, the government office moved to the new office compound in the West Garden area and the town was upgraded to a city. In the meantime, the government implemented a new ranking system for all government workers. Daddy was ranked 18th grade[27] with a salary of 108 *Yuan* RMB per month (As a comparison, the rice was 0.07 *Yuan* per pound at that time).

One thing impressed me the most was that when he received his salary, the first thing he did was to go to the post office, sending 20 *Yuan* to my grandparents.

It would take Daddy 40 minutes each way to go to the new office. Soon, the city put some government owned used bicycles for sale. Daddy bought a bicycle of "Forever" brand for 80 *Yuan* RMB (a brand new one would cost 120 *Yuan*), produced by the Shanghai Bicycle Company, one of the two Chinese bicycle companies at that time.[28]

---

[27] In China, the government cadre were ranked from 1 to 26 with the rank 1 the highest.

[28] The other bicycle company is Flying Pigeon. In February 1989, when President Bush and Barbara Bush visited China, they were given two Flying Pigeon bicycles as gifts.

The bicycle immediately became my favorite toy. After Daddy was back from his office, I took it over and tried to ride it. I used the rear rack as my seat so that my feet could touch the ground. Daddy told me: "whenever you feel that you are about to fall on one side, then make a turn on this side." Following his tip and with more practice, I was able to ride the bicycle. Then I helped my brother to learn it.

Another important event was that China had domestically produced the first truck, with the help from the Soviet Union. It was branded as the "Liberation." It is one of the accomplishments in the first Five Year Plan. The news was repeatedly broadcasted. In addition, there were poems, songs, and cartoons to praise it.

Soon, a Liberation truck arrived for demonstration. We were organized to watch it slowly moving through the main streets. The truck was decorated with a thick red belt around the top of the driver's cab, and its center had a silk flower just above the windshield. Some people stand on the cargo bed, beating the drums and cymbals. Everybody was proud of this great achievement.

As usual, the new school year started on September 1. Newly admitted students were organized into four classes, 50 students each. Like in elementary school, each class had one Teacher-in-Charge. Now, in middle school, some student monitors were appointed by the Teacher-in-Charge for helping with various aspects. There were five student monitors: the class leader and the deputy, who would help the Teacher-in-Charge for general matters; the study monitor, for study related issues; the sports monitor, for P.E. related activities; the entertainment monitor, for things related to entertaining, among other things, buying discount group movie tickets.

In the middle school, in addition to most classes in elementary school, the science class was split into Biology, Physics, and Chemistry. The Mathematics was split into Algebra and Plane Geometry. In Chinese literature class we started to learn newly published *Pinyin*. In the elementary school, we learned the phonetic symbol "*Bopomofo*," which is still used in Taiwan. Also, we started learning the simplified Chinese characters, which were published in January, 1956. In the Mainland China, we are probably the last generation who learned the traditional Chinese characters in the elementary school. Later, only the simplified Chinese characters are taught.

Like the literature textbook in the elementary school, there were many lessons related to the Korean War. One such a lesson was the article written by a well-known Chinese military reporter Mr. *Wei Wei*. The tittle of his article is "Who Are the Most Lovable Men,"[29] published in 1951. We were required to learn this lesson by heart. Our teacher explained that by describing various scenes, Mr. *Wei* praised the Chinese Volunteer Army's fiery hatred toward enemies and strong love toward their motherland and the brotherly North Korean people.

The teacher also told us that upon reading this article, Chairman Mao ordered to distribute it to the whole Chinese army. Since then, this article had been in the textbook for Mao's era, and beyond. In some provinces, this is still in the textbook.

Nadam Fair is a traditional Mongolian gathering, held every four years, mainly for entertaining. During the fair, Mongolian people would wear their traditional clothes, and come for horse racing, wrestling, archery, etc.

There was a *Nadam* fair held in the fall of 1956 near B-city. We were organized to participate, and were brought to the site by trucks. After the opening ceremony, we watched some horse race, wrestling, and archery competitions. There were many small vendors setting up tents there to sell drinks and various snacks. It was quite an eye-opening event.

Our middle school had a mimeographed student publication. All writings were contributed by students. Those, whose writings were accepted for publication, would be rewarded with pencils. Loving literature and writing, I tried to send some articles, and more often than not, my articles were accepted.

Then, I ventured to write a short novel. After finishing my initial draft, I gave it to Daddy and told him that I was interested in writing and wanted to be a writer. He read my manuscript carefully for a couple of days, and then talked to me. He praised my work briefly, then said that writing career could be treacherous, because there were literary inquisitions in history. Some intellectuals were executed, simply because of what they wrote. He told me some stories about this.

One such a story was during the Qing dynasty (1636-1912). While

---

[29]   This article is still available on the Internet.

a student was studying, a breeze came and turned the pages of his book. He joked:

"*Qing Feng bu shi zi, He Bi Luan fan Shu* (The light wind does not know a word, why do you turn my book)?"

Since *Qing* Dynasty was founded by the *Man* minority nationality whose language was not Chinese, and the Chinese character *Qing*, used as the adjective to the wind, sounded the same as the name of the dynasty, this student's poem was regarded as a roundabout way to attack the royal court, whose native language was not Chinese. As a result, this student was jailed.

So, Daddy recommended that I pursue a career in science, medicine, or engineering, which were much safer professions. From then on, I stopped sending my writings to that student publication, and paid more attention to science related classes.

Entering 1957, the last year of the first Five Year Plan in China, the economy improved significantly. In such a favorable situation, we celebrated Chinese New Year.

Traditionally, this is the most important family banquet of the year. Usually Mama cooked meals for us. Now Daddy also joined Mama preparing a traditional dinner of our home town in southern China. First, some potatoes blocks were laid down at the bottom of the wok. Then cooked chicken blocks, meat balls, small egg dumplings, rice noodles were put into the wok layer by layer. Finally, the chicken broth was poured in. After that, the wok was put on the stove to heat up. When the soup was boiling, Daddy put the wok on the center of the dining table, and the New Year's Eve dinner started. Daddy liked *Baijiu*, the Chinese liquor. He also bought a small bottle of grape wine for us three kids. In cold winter, with such warm food, liquor, and wine, the holiday atmosphere was especially jubilant. We all enjoyed the dinner enormously.

Indeed, this is one of the most memorable Chinese New Year's Eves in my life.

During the spring break in 1957, the school organized the first grade of the middle school to travel to a well-known Lama Temple: The South Temple, which was about ten miles south of B-city. With our luggage carried by a truck, we all walked a long way to the temple. We had one break for every hour, and ate homemade steamed bread for lunch. It took us about 5 hours to get there. The temple was at the foot of the west side of the H-mountain. We were divided into groups of 7 – 10 students each, and lived in the temple's guest rooms.

Next day, we went to see the main hall of the temple after breakfast. The hall was like a small theater. There was a gold-foil covered real body of a lama, and this body was regarded as a Buddha. On the opposite side, there were two stairways leading to the second floor, which was built along back and two side walls, much like the second floor of a theater.

Climbing into the second floor, our teacher started to explain the temple. While he was speaking, a lama came up and whispered something to our teacher. Then the teacher said: "All female students, please leave the hall." Later we learned that the lama told our teacher that females in the hall were offensive to the Buddha, i.e., the gold-foil covered lama's body. After that, only boys were allowed to enter the hall. This made those girls resentful.

After lunch, we went to climb the H-Mountain. There were a lot of pine and cypress trees. When climbing to the height where there were still un-melted ice and snow, we stopped. At that place, we have a much better view of the west desert. There were spotted small green areas in the yellow sand dunes, made the scene spectacular under the setting sun.

A few weeks after the travel, a comet was showing up on the north-west of the sky in the evenings, visible by naked eyes. The comet was called *Saozhou Xing* (broom star) in Chinese, because it looks like a broom.

According to old books and dramas, the appearance of a comet was a bad omen: once it appeared, some disasters would follow. For weeks, the Central Radio Station, newspapers, and magazines published articles to explain that the appearance of the comet was a natural phenomenon. People were advised not do believe this old superstition. This was the first time in my life to see a comet.

One day in our summer vacation, I saw a group of people gathered in Under-the-Big-Tree. I thought there was some show by travelling salesmen, and went to take a look. There was a young man standing at the center of the crowd with two middle-aged men standing on his sides, and a couple of other people behind him. About 30-40 onlookers gathered there. One of the middle-aged men, holding a tall white paper hat with the words "*youpai fengzi* (the rightist)", announced that this young man was a rightist, and put the paper hat on his head. The young man took off the hat immediately, and said he was no a rightist. That middle-aged man, apparently angry, grabbed the hat and put it back on forcefully. In the meantime, other fellows helped to hold the young man's arms. Not able to move, tears started to flow from his eyes. I had never seen such a violent scene and was scared. So, I walked away hurriedly.

Soon, I heard from my former classmates that Mr. *Li*, who had taught us Chinese literature in elementary school, became a rightist.

"Why is that?" I asked.

"He responded to the call to criticize the communist party and he did just that. But later, he was denounced as a rightist."

I could not believe this rumor until I saw Mr. *Li* in the street some days later. According to the school rules for students, whenever we saw a teacher or former teacher outside the school, we must greet and bow to the teacher. Normally the teacher would nod and smile. But this time, when I greeted him, Mr. *Li* turned his head away, pretending not to see me, and walked away. This confirmed that Mr. *Li* had indeed become a rightist. Recalling the scene that I saw in Under-the-Big-Tree, and gazing at his receding figure, I felt strong compassion toward him.

As usual, our new school year started on Sept. 1. It was the second year in the junior high. I joined the line for receiving new textbooks outside the school's warehouse. When I entered the room, I saw our Dean of Education was distributing textbooks, something he never did before. I was puzzled. Then I overheard some students saying that the dean was denounced as a rightist during the summer vacation, and was deprived of his post.

After the new semester started, I heard more news about the anti-rightist campaign. It was a nationwide campaign, not just in this city. Many well-known writers, poets, such as *Ding Ling, Feng Xuefeng, Fu Lei, Wang Meng*, etc., were denounced as rightists.

In spring 1957, the Communist Party of China (CPC) called on people to criticize the party, and those who ventured to criticize were encouraged and praised at first. But then the wind reversed in the summer. As a result, those who stick their necks out to criticize the Party were labeled as "rightists," and suffered from demotion, decreased salary, to sending to labor camps. It was said that each unit must dig out about 5 percent of total employees as rightists. Some rightists tried to protest, saying:

"It was the Party that asked us to criticize, why we were now criminalized?"

The answer was that this was the strategy of "luring the snake out of the den." This way, the hidden class enemies would expose themselves so that they could be eliminated easily.

In October 1957, the Soviet Union successfully launched Sputnik, the first satellite in human history. The state media enthusiastically reported this news, saying this was not only the great achievement of the Soviet Union, but also the great achievement of the socialist camp headed by the Soviet Union.

The official media further praised this as the proof that the socialism[30] was far superior to the capitalism.

This mass propaganda also had an additional effect: to make *Wei Xing* (Chinese word for satellite) popular, and used figuratively to mean a great achievement.

1958 was known as the year of the Big Leap Forward. There were a lot of big posters of "Go all out, aim high, and achieve greater, faster, better, and more economical results in building socialism." More loudspeakers were installed on the electric poles and roofs of buildings. A new song "Socialism Is Good" was repeatedly played via those loudspeakers. Soon we learned the lyrics by heart:

> Socialism is good, socialism is good!
> People in socialist countries are highly respected.
> Counter-revolutionists had fallen down;

---

[30] Different from the one used in the West, the term "socialism" used in communist countries is defined as the primary stage of the communist, according the Marxism theory.

The imperialists were all gone.
United our whole country,
Let's move the tide of the socialist construction to new
heights!

In the spring of 1958, there was another campaign: Wipe out Four
Pests (Mice, Flies, Mosquitoes, and Sparrows). We were organized to watch
some newsreels about the best techniques used by people in other parts
of the country. The one impressed me the most was a mass movement to
exhaust sparrows. People used long bamboo poles and anything that could
produce a loud noise, such as drums, symbols, basin, or even woks, as well
as shouting loudly to disturb and scare sparrows. The sparrows had to keep
flying from one place to the other until they were exhausted. Then the
sparrows would fall to the ground like raining.

Based on my knowledge of geography, the Soviet Union and Mongolia
were our northern neighbors. So, unless they also had the same campaign
to wipe out the four pests, the flies and sparrows could fly across the
borders. How could we act alone to eliminate the four pests? However,
when I asked Daddy, he warned me again that this was one of the most
dangerous questions to ask. I could become a rightist or even a counter-
revolutionist by asking a question like this. Recalling the sense that I saw
in Under-the-Big-Tree, my former teacher *Li*, and our dean of education,
I was scared, and no longer talking about this campaign.

For us young students, the task was focused on wiping out flies. Since
it was spring time, we were told to dig out and destroy the pupae. We
would go to the areas where there were large number of pupae, such as the
public latrines and its vicinity, to pick up them. When we turned them
in, the pupae would be weighed and the weight of the pupae would be
recorded as the indication of our accomplishments.

This was a boring and slow process. Some fellows found a more
efficient way. Bringing some spades and bamboo dustpans, they shove
the pupa-rich dirt into the dustpan. Some other students would bring the
dustpan to the nearby creek to pan the mixture. The dirt would be washed
away, and the pupae, empty hatched pupae shells, grasses, and broken
tree branches would be left in the dustpan. Not sure how this mix would
be weighed and counted, I followed them to the collecting station. As it

turned out, the mix was weighed, accepted, and counted the same way as the dry and unhatched ones.

Next day, I followed suit. Soon we finished our tasks with flying colors.

One day, Mr. *Yao*, our Teacher-in-Charge, started a discussion about the classical poem and the modern poem. Influenced by my early experience with classical poems, I said I liked the classical poems better. I did not expect this simple class discussion would get me into trouble. In the next class, one of my classmates started to attack me by saying that my thought was reactionary. Then he read a revolutionary poem "Ode to *Yan-an*".[31] After that he claimed that this poem was a thousand times better than the poems by *Li Bai, Du Fu, and Bai Juyi*, three most famous poets in *Tang* Dynasty (618-907 A.D.). When I raised my hand and wanted to debate, Mr. *Yao* did not give me a chance. Instead, he allowed others with the same opinion as this classmate to continue criticizing me.

When I told Daddy about this incident, he said that it was likely due to that Chairman Mao recently advocated a phrase "*Hou Jin Bo Gu* (put higher priority on the present and lower priority on the ancient)." By quoting the old Chinese saying, "The disease comes in via the mouth, and the disaster comes out of the mouth," Daddy reminded me of the literary inquisition we discussed earlier. He emphasized that saying anything wrong, at the wrong moment, or at the wrong place, could cause trouble or even disasters. He suggested that I do a self-criticism in the next class.

I followed his advice and avoided further trouble.

As Big Leap Forward was going more broadly, every section of the society was trying to "launch big satellite," or making great achievements. During that time, I frequently saw somebody wearing handcuffs and escorted by policemen in the street. This was a scene that I had never seen before.

In the morning on June 23, it was not clear why I felt very hard to concentrate, and wished the class to end soon. Finally, the morning classes were finished. Upon entering the yard, Mama came out and stopped me. I was astonished by her ashen face. She showed me a search warrant, and said that some policemen were searching our home.

I noticed the charge on the warrant was "historical counter-revolutionist,

---

[31]   *Yan-an* was the revolutionary base of the CPC from 1935 – 1949.

because he worked in the KMT government as a county mayor in 1941-1942." I asked what the historical counter-revolutionist was, Mama explained that this means someone acted against the Communist Party before the Liberation. Then she said in a very low voice:

"It does not make sense to charge your Daddy this way. From 1936 to 1945, the KMT and the CPC were in the United Front against Japanese invaders. The two parties were partners not enemies, when your Daddy worked in the KMT government. Moreover, when the B-town was peacefully liberated, the so-called "*ji wan bu Jiu* (in the future, no action would be pursued against their past background) policy of the central government was announced to those who joined the peaceful liberation. Now that promise was also breached. Unfortunately, after the Liberation, lawyer profession was eliminated, there was no way for us to find a lawyer[32] to defend your Daddy."

Upon hearing this, I was infuriated by the injustice, and wanted to argue with those policemen. But Mama grabbed me firmly, and warned: "They have guns, and could shoot you quickly!" I gave up in despair, and suddenly remembered the window fire on the first night we arrived at B-town. It was indeed an unfortunate omen!

I felt my mouth extremely dry, and could not swallow anything. I did not eat lunch and went to school like a dream walker, without any memory of how I got into the classroom. In the whole afternoon, the episodes I spent with Daddy, were like movies in my head. When I came back from the school in the late afternoon, Mama said the policemen had taken away all the letters, silver coins, especially the photo albums, which had great sentimental value to our family (All these items have never been returned to us). Several weeks later, the public security department, i.e., the police department,[33] sent us a notice saying that Daddy was brought to the LT-county, where he had served as a county mayor. He would be tried there.

In the past, Mama rarely talked about the history of our family, because we were too young to understand. After Daddy's arrest, Mama started to tell us more.

Daddy was born on February 10, 1907, and Mama was born on

---

[32] Lawyer profession was restored in 1979 after the Cultural Revolution.

[33] In China, the public security department is equivalent to the police department.

October 22, 1910. According to the old tradition, their marriage was arranged by their parents, and engaged when they were very young.

After graduating from middle school, Daddy applied to, and was accepted by the Department of Economics at *Jinan* University in Shanghai. This university was founded in *Qing* Dynasty, and was one of the top universities in China. A devout Christian, my maternal grandma sent Mama to a Christian elementary school, running by some American missionaries, and she also became a devout Christian. After graduating from high school, Mama also attended *Jinan* University, majoring in Education.

Upon graduating with a B.S. Degree in 1929, Daddy found a teaching position in a middle school in *Nanjing*. Mama also found a teaching job in an elementary school in *Nanjing* after receiving an associate degree in Education. They were married in 1930. In 1931 my elder brother was born. Later, Mama gave birth to two more daughters. Due to her workload, she could only keep my elder brother with her. My two sisters stayed with my maternal grandma in her home town: Y-town.

In 1937, the War of Resistance against Japanese Aggression started. One of Daddy's university classmates wrote a letter to Daddy, inviting him to work in G-province, the rear area at that time, where the government badly needed well-educated people. Daddy was growing up in southeast area of China, where it had nice climate, was more populated, and prosperous. Whereas the west region was less populated, and less developed. The living conditions were poor, and the winter was long and cold.

However, facing the foreign invasion, Daddy was determined to help the government and serve the homeland in any way he could. He bade goodbye to Mama and three young children, and left for G-province. Daddy was very able and worked hard. In a couple of years, he was promoted from an ordinary office worker to the Mayor of LT- County, when he was only in his early 30s. He was so patriotic that he lived frugally to set an example for his subordinates. At the end of 1941, the county government saved more than 1000 lbs. of food, and he donated the saved food to the central government for fighting the Japanese aggressors.

However, he soon realized that political arena was too treacherous, and wanted to go back to his major: economics.

While in G-province, he met Mongolia prince *Dalizhaya* and they became good friends. Knowing Daddy had a B. S. Degree in Economics from the famous *Jinan* University, the prince cordially invited Daddy to join his trading company. Daddy quitted the mayor job in 1942 to work for the prince, and was appointed as the director of L-city office of the Alxa Trade Company.

Because of the poor medical facilities during the war time, my two sisters, who lived with my grandma, died of diseases. One of them was 10 years old, and had attended elementary school. Mama choked with tears when mentioning these heartbreaking events. The events made her stop working, and raising children became her top priority, after I was born.

In 1949, Daddy was one of the prince's representatives to negotiate peacefully liberate B-town, where the prince's palace and the headquarter of his trading company were located. Mama reminded me that when we were fleeing the battle in 1949, we saw Daddy off with a dozen other people. That was the time when they went to negotiate with the representatives from the PLA. Daddy kept a red banquet invitation card with *Xi Zhongxun's* [34] signature on it. This card was also taken away by the policemen when the policemen searched our home, and never returned to us.

Since all the peaceful liberation actions were regarded as the meritorious contribution to the new China, Prince *Dalizhaya* was appointed as the head of the new local government and a vice chairman of the Inner Mongolia Autonomous Region, [35] and Daddy was arranged to work in the transportation department. An important policy of the central government was announced to those who joined the peaceful liberation: in the future no action would be pursued against their past background, or "*ji wan bu jiu*" in Chinese.

After I was born, Daddy gave me the name, which means to garrison the LT-county. I never expect that my name could cause trouble.

After entering the middle school, I was befriended by a classmate, whose last name happened to be the same as mine. He quoted the folk saying "those, who have the same last name, were in the same family 500

---

[34] He was the political commissar of the North-West Military Region and B-town was in this territory. His son Xi Jinping is the president of China since 2012.

[35] Prince *Dalizhaya* suffered badly in the Cultural Revolution, and died on site in 1968 during a mass denouncing rally.

years ago," and said that we were brothers. I helped him numerous times with his homework, and we frequently played together.

After Daddy's arrest, he reported to our Techer-in-Charge, saying my father gave me this name because he wanted me to continue ruling the people of the LT-county. Our Techer-in-Charge wrote this in my yearly review, and asserted that I wanted to follow my counter-revolutionary father's steps.

After reading my yearly review, Mama changed my given name.

Without Daddy's monthly 108 RMB salary, our family immediately fell into financial difficulties. However, I did not see Mama dropping a single tear, nor did I hear she said any depressing words. She frequently prayed, asking the Lord to give her the serenity to accept the things that she cannot change, and to give her the wisdom to do whatever she can, to overcome all the difficulties.

Indeed, Mama had demonstrated her iron-will and great courage to face all the hardship. Since Daddy's arrest, his friends had been avoiding us like the plague. When meeting in the street and I greeted them as before, they would ignore me as if they had never known me. Our grandfather and my father's brothers and sisters also stopped contacting us.

However, the two brothers of my mother demonstrated great compassion towards us, and were willing to help. Mama's elder brother, a profession in H-province Teacher's Institute, sent letters to console us, and also sent some money to help us financially. Mama's younger brother, who was a professor in Beijing Iron and Steel Institute, expressed the willingness to take my younger brother to live with them.

My elder brother graduated from the Medical Institute of S-province in 1956, and assigned a job as a doctor in the Hospital in H-city. Mama wrote a letter to tell him what had happened. After some discussion, they decided that we would go to H-city to live with him for the time being. Then my younger brother would go to Beijing to live with the younger uncle.

To prepare for the travel, Mama sold the household items, including the bicycle that both my younger brother and I loved so much. Near the end of August, we sold most of the items and left B-town.

We took long distance bus to Y-city where there was a railway station.

After one hour or so, the driver stopped the bus on the road side. Getting off the bus, we noticed the front wheel on the right side dropped away. At first some passengers thought that was because the nuts holding the wheel were loose. But after a close look, we realized that it was the front shaft that had broken, and that it could not be repaired quickly.

There was no way to contact B-town station because there was no telephone box along the road. Moreover, there were only a few automobiles travelling on this road. We waited more than an hour to see a truck coming from Y-city. Our driver waived to the truck, and asked the driver to report the problem so that another bus could be dispatched to carry us to Y-city.

In the late afternoon, we saw a truck coming to take us, because there was no more bus available. After a short trip, the engine stalled. The truck driver and our bus driver checked the engine, and discovered that the battery and the charging system were not working properly. But they tried their best to continue driving on and off with many stops. Normally it took three hours to get to Y-city from where our bus stopped. But when we finally arrived at our destination, it was well passed the midnight. As it turned out, this traveling experience was another miserable omen for the years to come.

H-city (1958-1960)

At the hotel, Mama asked me whether I could take care of my younger brother and sister for a couple of days so that she could go to LT-county and see Daddy.

"Yes, I can," I answered.

However, after some hesitation, she decided not to go.

"Why," I asked,

She told me that I had not yet been 15, my younger brother had been less than 12, and my sister had been just past 9. We were too young to live independently. In case something happened to any of us, she would feel guilty.

After losing two daughters, she believed that this choice was what Daddy would also want.

Boarding the train, we left for H-city. The section of the railroad from Y-city to H-city was newly built, and just started a test operation. There were not many passengers. So, we were able to sleep on the bench at night.

Waking up in the next morning, we found the train had stopped. The bridge in front of us had not finished laying the rail, so we had to walk over the bridge to board another train for the next leg.

After arriving in H-city, we stayed in my eldest brother's small dormitory for singles. A few days later, my younger brother went to Beijing to live with our younger uncle's family.

In the meantime, Mama brought me to several nearby middle schools to see whether some school still had a vacancy. Finally, the *Hui* Middle school accepted me, and I started the third year in junior high. This school was located in the areas where there were a large number of *the Hui people*, a minority nationality. Islam is part of their culture. In this school, about a half of the students were of *Hui* nationality, and the rest were of *Han*.

With the experience I gained in B-city to get along with Mongolian classmates, I was able to quickly make friends with *Hui* students. Actually, *Hui* nationality does not have their own language, and they all speak Chinese. From those *Hui* classmates, I learned a lot about their religion and customs, such as Ramadan.

The courses and textbooks were the same as the ones in the First Middle school of B-city. Our music teacher was newly graduated, and just started teaching. He was very enthusiastic. In one class, after finishing the required materials, he pulled out a violin and played a piece of music. It was wonderful! He asked whether we want to learn, most of the students eagerly raised their hands, including me. He taught us how to hold the violin and the bow, and how to move the bow on the four strings. Then he asked us to practice during the afternoon's free activity time.

There was a lab in our school with various music instruments. In the afternoon, the students, who were interested in violin, went to the lab to borrow violins for practice. As instructed, we started bowing on the open E string for the day. Next day, we were asked to play the open A string. I noticed that more than a half of the students did not come. On the third day, when we were asked to play the open D string, I was the only one there. Next afternoon, I found the lab window was closed. After waiting for a while, there seemed still no one coming to open the lab. I went to see my music teacher and asked why there was nobody in the music lab. He told me that since there were too few students interested, he decided to cancel the extracurricular violin class. Upon hearing this, I was very disappointed.

I looked the section of music instruments in the department store near the school. The cheapest violin was 60 *Yuan* RMB, which was about my elder brother's monthly salary -- too expensive. Then I attempted to build a violin myself. I borrowed a book about how to build a violin from the city's public library. With limited tools, I tried to use paper for the top and bottom plates by glue many layers of paper together. But when I put strings on it, and tightened only two strings, the paper violin bent like a bow. I gave up.

In 1958, the central government proposed a new slogan: *Zhengzhi Guashuai,* which literally means "politics[36] would be the marshal." Actually, this slogan means the politics is of the foremost importance, and should have the number one priority. So political class was added in our curriculum. Since the textbook had not been written on this subject, the teacher used the newspapers, especially the People's Daily, as his source of the information.

During the class, the teacher explained the current policies of the central government and about the situations and important events in China as well as in the world. During the Big Leap Forward, the People's Commune had started in the countryside, and cities also started to follow the lead. In such a situation, our teacher started discussions to prepare us for the upcoming People's Commune. In some classes he asked students to talk about what they knew about this topic. One student, who was interested in politics, said that two important features of the People's Commune were large and collective. Based on these features, our school could be a people's commune. We all would live together. There would be no family because according the Engels, the family was the origin of private properties, which was in conflict with the collective principle. Our fathers and mothers would be our comrades. To see them, we might need the permit, issued by our People's Commune, like applying for a passport.

The teacher did not say anything about this point of view. He just let other students say whatever in their mind. But after the anti-rightist campaign, people realized that improper words could bring disasters, so the discussion fell into silence. Several students said that the related materials were hard to understand, and that we had read very little. Most students agreed. So, the teacher gave us more materials to read.

However, weeks had passed, our school did not establish the People's Commune, and everyone continued to lead their lives as before.

In addition, there was another campaign "*Quan Min Jie Bing* (every citizen is a soldier)." There was a poster showing a militiaman with a rifle in his back and fly swatter in his hand aiming towards an American soldier at the size of a fly. The caption showed a poem:

---

[36] In China, the meaning of the word "politics" is different than its meaning in the West. Its meaning is close to ideology.

Six hundred million people in the nation,
Everyone is a soldier,
Fighting the American guys,
Just like swatting a fly.

To implement Every-Citizen-is-a-Soldier, the school organized military training. In addition to various military formations, we were taught to use the small-caliber rifle. At the end, we were given five bullets for practice. Due to my good eyesight, I was able to hit the center of the target 5 times in a row. A girl, who had never even played a toy gun, was scared. Each time she fired a shot, her body would jerk, which caused other students to laugh. As a result, she missed the target in all her five shots.

During the high gear period of Big Leap Forward in 1958, every day the newspapers would report "launching fantastic satellite" somewhere in China. A photo even showed that the rice in the field was growing so densely that several children could stand on top of the crops. One of the most popular slogans was: "*yi tian deng yu 20 nian*! (Make the achievements of 20 years in one day)." A poem reflected the people's euphoric spirit at that time:

There is no *Yu* Emperor in the heaven,[37]
There is no Dragon King in the ocean.[38]
We are the *Yu* Emperor;
We are the Dragon King!
Order the mountains to get out of our way,
We are coming!

In response to the Party's campaign for producing 10,700,000 tons of steel, the target of 1958, our school built a couple of backyard blast furnaces in October. Classes were suspended and all students lived in our classrooms, working three shifts a day to make iron.

Students were divided into groups with 10 students in each group. My

---

[37] According to the Chinese fairy tales, there is an emperor, *Yu Huang*, in the heaven, who governs gods and goddesses.

[38] The Chinese fairy tales say there is a dragon king in the ocean.

group's task was to prepare the raw materials. We would weigh iron ores, charcoals, and limestones, based on some given proportion, and put them into baskets, which would be picked up by a different group, and lifted to the platform near the top of the furnace. Then the group of students on the platform would pour them into the furnace at certain time intervals. Several hours later, another group would open the hole for the slag, which was near the bottom of the furnace, to let the slag flow out. After that, this hole would be plugged. Then, the opening of the iron, which was lower than the slag hole, would be opened. When the first time the liquid iron flew out of the opening, we were all excited and cheered.

Next day, some people would weigh the cooled iron blocks and record the weight.

With so many young people living in the classrooms, it was fun and relaxed when we were not in the working shift. Telling stories was a major way of passing time. Mr. *Luo*, my classmate, was a good story-teller, and he seemed to have an infinite number of funny stories in his head. One such story was about monks. An old monk and a child monk lived in a temple in a mountain. Over the years, the old monk repeatedly told the little monk:

"Women were tigers, which would eat people. So, we should stay away from them."

When the child monk grew up, the old monk decided to bring him to the nearest town to learn the life of the real world. Entering the town, they saw many shops and stalls. That was really an eye-opening experience for the young monk. Then, they saw a beautiful girl coming. Never seeing a female before, the young monk asked:

"What is this?"

"A tiger," the master answered, "one of people-eating tigers that I have told you many times before."

However, upon seeing the girl, the young monk totally forgot the warnings by his master, and kept watching her until she walked out of sight. Returning to the temple, the master asked the young monk what he liked the most during this trip.

"The tiger." The young monk answered without a hesitation.

Upon hearing this, everybody laughed loudly.

Recalling this story many times later, it seems to indicate that brainwashing would eventually fail, when the reality comes in.

After a month or so, our school received a notice from the government, ordering us to stop our backyard furnaces. This was to ensure that the big and high-quality steel companies could get sufficient raw materials. Indeed, because the iron-making process in the backyard furnace was hard to control, the cast iron we produced contained high sulfur and phosphorus, and was basically useless. I saw the piled iron blocks starting to rust in the yard. After our iron-producing work stopped, the classes restarted, and our school was back to normal. In the early 1959, the newspaper announced that the goal of making 10,700,000 tons of steel had been successfully accomplished.

In our physics class, the teacher mentioned the ore radio set, which uses a piece of pyrites to detect the radio signal, and told us that some books and magazines had more detailed information.

The materials were inexpensive, so I decided to build one. After several days, the receiver was finished. Wearing a set of headphones, I was able to hear the radio broadcast. Fascinated by this, I became a radio amateur.

One day my older brother brought a young student, Mr. *Meng*, to our home, and introduced him to me. He was a student in his second year in the senior high school, and was my brother's patient. When visiting my brother's office, he brought a magazine "Radio." Knowing I was also a radio amateur, my brother thought it would be a good idea to let us know each other. We quickly became friends. Mr. *Meng* suggested that I apply the same school that he was attending, because there was a club for the student radio amateur.

After passing the entrance examination at the end of the spring semester, I applied and admitted by that school.

During the summer vacation, my brother married his fiancée, who just graduated from the medical institute where my brother also attended. They spent their honeymoon in his wife's parents' home in Shanghai. So, I was alone in H-city.

Mr. *Meng* told me that Beijing Vacuum Tube Factory was selling the amateur-grade vacuum tubes, which did not pass their QC, but was usable for amateurs. The price was about 30-40 percent lower than the regular ones. This was great news. At such an affordable price, I was able to buy a set of amateur grade tubes for a radio set. With help from Mr. Meng, I built a bare-bone radio set, i.e., without a housing, and presented it as a gift for my brother's wedding. With the short waves, we could receive many foreign broadcasts. At that time, the only foreign radio program "Moscow-Beijing," broadcasted by the Soviet Union in Mandarin, was allowed for Chinese people to listen. It was a crime to listening to the so-called enemy stations, such as Voice of America, and other stations from the so-called Imperialistic Camp.[39]

We were told that the public security department could detect who was listening to the enemies' stations, and punish them heavily. But we did not believe this was possible. Without emitting any signal, how could they know what we were receiving? So, sometimes we ventured to listen to the "enemy" stations by wearing headphones, and had never been detected.

After several months, Mama still could not find a proper job in H-city, she decided to bring my younger sister to return to N-city in J-province, where most our relatives and friends lived. It could be easier to find a job with the help from them. I continued to stay with my elder brother for the time being.

In early September, I started my first year in senior high school, and joined the amateur radio club. In addition to the courses we had studied in the junior high, Russian, a new foreign language course, was added. During the honeymoon time of 1950s, the Soviet Union was the Big Brother and the head of the communist camp. So, we must study its language in order to learn from the Soviet Union.

Our Russian teacher just graduated from the Beijing Foreign Language Institute and was taught by Soviet professors. After we gained some basic knowledge and vocabulary, our Russian teacher taught us how to sing "The East is Red" in Russian, and some other Russian songs, such as "Moscow Nights."

In the senior high school, in addition to the student monitors, each class also had a branch of Communist Youth League, with a Secretary, a Head of Organization, and a Head of Propaganda. They would accept some politically active students as new members.

Influenced by the "Big Leap Forward," our school started some

---

[39]   This camp included all Western countries, Taiwan, and Hong Kong.

experiments, one of which was to teach college courses. Analytic Geometry was added to our curriculum. Also, several classes were set to be the "Leap Forward Class," which would finish three-year courses in two years. The students of the "Leap Forward Class" would graduate one year earlier.[40]

Meanwhile, to implement the new educational principles of "Education Should Serve Proletarian Politics" and "Education Should be in Connection to Production," our school bought some machine tools so that students can practice manufacturing first-handedly. I was assigned to operate the lathe.

Since the machine tools were limited and there were too many students, we could only put our hands on the machines one hour for each week.

Inventions were highly encouraged. A device, ultra-sonic water heater, was said to be an energy-saving invention. It was made of a used bullet shell. Sawing off the bottom of the shell, and hammering the front opening to make it near flat, then we would insert a piece of a used double-sided razor blade. After securing the piece of the blade, we produced an ultra-sonic water heater.

When using it, we would connect the bottom to a tube, which provided water vapor, and put the heater into a water-filled container. We were told that when the vapor passing thought the flat part of the device, the razor blade would produce ultra-sonic vibration, and heat the water much quicker than the coal stove. Some of us were not sure the device was effective, because it seemed to us that the water vapor along could also heat the water. So, the claim of saving energy was not convincing, unless we could set up the experiment to compare the two cases, where one with the device and one without it.

But again, it could be politically dangerous to propose such an experiment, because the invention was reported as the achievement of the Big Leap Forward. To suspect such an achievement could bring troubles, like the ones in the anti-rightist campaign.

October 1, 1959, was the tenth anniversary of the founding of the People's Republic of China. People were enthusiastically preparing for the celebration. While walking to my school, I noticed some organizations, with the front door facing the street, installed temporary light poles. On

---

[40]   In China, the elementary school has 6 school years, junior and senior high school have 3 school years each.

September 30, after it was dark, those lights were turned on, the people in those organizations started the Soviet-style group dancing. Next morning, when I went out for a morning walk, I saw some people still dancing. They had danced overnight to express their love to the new China, and the Party.

One day, our Teacher-in-Charge called a meeting. During the meeting, he asked us to report our *Jiating Chushen* (family background). In early 1950s, families in China were classified into different classes[41] based on their properties before the Liberation. According to the Marxist-Leninist theory, the rich families were exploitive. Therefore, the properties of the rich should be confiscated, and distributed to the poor. In the countryside the properties of two classes, the Landlord Class and the Rich Peasant Class, were confiscated and distributed to the poor. In cities, there were more categories of the family background. Those who owned a business were classified as the Capitalist Class. The capitalist was also one of the exploitive classes.

The teacher first asked those who were from the Landlord family to raise their hands, then he put some note on his student name list. Then, he asked the students from the Rich Peasant Class, the Capitalist Class, etc. to raise their hands, and made notes.

After that, he asked the remaining students about their family background. This was the first time I had ever heard about the term "family background," as did a few other students. We did not know what our family backgrounds were. The teacher asked us to find out, and report to him as soon as possible.

I asked my elder brother, he told me that our family background was the Clerk Class because Daddy was an office worker in the prince *Dalizhaya*'s trading company just before the Liberation.

One morning, when opening the drawer of my desk,[42] I was surprised to see that my Russian-Chinese dictionary disappeared. I asked who had borrowed it. Nobody. In the meantime, more students discovered that they also lost

---

[41]   The word "class" here means the group of people with some common features, based on Marxism-Leninism doctrine.

[42]   When I attended schools, every class had fixed classroom. A small desk was assigned to each student. We can leave our books and stationaries in the drawers of our desks.

things. So, we went to our Teacher-in-Charge to report this. The teacher told us that students from several other classes had also lost their belongings. The school reported the theft event to the public security department.

After a couple of months, one day a classmate rushed into the classroom and told us: "The thief is Mr. *Wei Zeyuan*! He is arrested." We were all astonished, because a couple of months before, he was awarded with a silk banner of recognition, in an all-hands meeting. During the meeting, the principal read a letter which was included in the same package as the silk banner.

According to the letter, the sender, a high-ranking officer of the Party, said that he was shopping in a department store where he fainted and fell down. It was Mr. *Wei*, who called a pedicab to send him to a hospital. After a doctor's treatment, Mr. *Wei* called another pedicab, accompanied him to his home, paid all the fees, and then left without leaving his name. The letter mentioned that the sender had only found *Wei*'s name by asking the hospital, where the Mr. *Wei*'s student ID was copied down when they checked in. He praised Mr. *Wei* as an unsung hero with the high communist morality.

How could such a hero become a thief? Everybody was puzzled. But we soon got the answer. The public security department sent an officer to our school to give us a report. He said that based on their investigation, the event in the department store was faked by Mr. *Wei*: there had been no such a senior officer. He told us that the lie had many flaws. For example, it was impossible for such a high-ranking officer to go out alone, they would be accompanied by their bodyguards. In addition, for such a high-ranking officer, the government would assign a car and a chauffeur for him or her. There was no need to hire a pedicab. Moreover, the silk banner package was sent via the post office. For such a high-ranking officer, it would be more natural for him to ask his chauffeur to deliver the package to our school.

He said that our school leaders could be so glad to see a high-ranking officer praising their student that they did not give this event a second thought.

In late 1959, necessaries of life showed the sign of shortage. In one of our political classes, a classmate asked why it was hard to buy light bulbs those days. Another student asked why we had no enough food. The teacher explained that due to the Big Leap Forward, we had built an unprecedented number of new houses, in such a situation, the shortage of light bulbs seemed understandable. Then a classmate asked why the light bulb factories had not made a Big Leap Forward? The teacher replied that the development could not be perfectly balanced. Some might be faster than others, just like our fingers, whose lengths were not equal.

As for the shortage of food, the teacher answered the question with a new question: "Our people's communes have launched so many satellites, how could we have no enough food?" He continued: "I think it is more related to the way you cook. For example, with a half kilograms of flour, you can make a pancake with the radius 10 cm, after eating it, three people might not feel full. But if you make a noodle soup out of the same amount of flour, that soup would surely fill the three stomachs!" We all laughed.[43]

During the early 1960, we had not received any letter from Mama for several weeks. My elder brother suspected that something might have gone wrong, and sent a telegram to Mama. She finally sent a letter telling us that Daddy had passed away. In her letter she also enclosed a notification from the prison authority saying that Daddy had died of a stomach ulcer on Feb 20, 1960[44]. He was 53.

In late 1959, we received a letter from Daddy which mentioned that Mama's letter was received, but the food package, mentioned in that letter, was not. That was the last letter we received from Daddy.

Since his arrest up to the time I lived in the United States, I have dreamed many times that Daddy had finished his prison term, and returned home. But when I woke up, I realized that they were just dreams. In the dreams, he looked the same as the time we lived together, even when my age passed 53 when dreaming.

In the summer vacation of 1960, I decided to join Mama. My elder brother bought a train ticket for me to go to N-city.

---

[43] As a result of the Big Leap Forward and establishing people's commune, a nationwide famine occurred.

[44] Later, we learned that during the great famine of 1960-1962, G-province, where my father was jailed, had one out of every four people died of starvation. It is quite possible that my father was one of those perished due to the famine. The central authority had been hide this information from the general public. Only in 21th century did some authors started to reveal the great famine, such as the book "Tombstone" by *Yang Jisheng* and Edward Friedman.

N-city (1960-1962)

The train went overnight, and then arrived *Yongding* Gate station of Beijing. My younger brother was there to meet me.

"Daddy had passed away" was the first words he said.

Tears were full of four eyes immediately. But we dared not to cry out loudly because Daddy was charged as a historical counter-revolutionist, or a class enemy. To mourn a class enemy could bring us troubles.

To facilitate attending school, my uncle bought a monthly bus pass for my brother. He made a good use of it by traveling a lot on Sundays, and became a living map of Beijing. Now he acted as my guide. After some transfers, we arrived at the Beijing Institute of Iron and Steel. This institute was built with the help from the Soviet Union in the early 1950s, and specialized in Metallurgical industry. Graduates would be assigned jobs in this industry.

Entering the big front gate, there was a Soviet-style main building. Passing this building, I saw a large sports field. My uncle's house was located beside this field.

I had met my uncle and aunt briefly in N-city in the early 1950s, but it was the first time that I had ever seen three of my uncle's four children. The eldest was attending *Qing Hua* (Tsinghua) University and lived in the university's student dormitory. She was busy with her study, and rarely came home. I did not meet her this time.

My brother was attending Beijing 101 Middle School, one of the famous middle schools in Beijing. He shared a bedroom with one of the cousins. I also saw my maternal grandma again, who had been living with my younger uncle after we left N-city in 1953.

After a short stay, my brother saw me off in the new Beijing Railway

Station, one of the ten construction projects for the tenth anniversary of the founding of the People's Republic of China. In that railway station, I saw the escalator the first time in my life, and was amazed by its operation.

I continued my travel via Shanghai and arrived at my destination: N-city railway station. My younger sister and Small *Lu* received me at the station. I had not seen Small *Lu* for seven years. He had grown from a boy to a tall young man, and was studying at J-province Engineering Institute, majoring in chemical engineering.

My sister had also grown taller. I noticed that she was wearing a pair of light cyan shoes made by Mama. Traditionally, wearing shoes made of white cloth is a way of mourning their parents who passed away recently. Since Daddy passed away in the prison with the charge of historical counter-revolutionist, Mama thought it was not a good idea to wear white shoes, fearing the "Resident Committee"[45] might find fault with us. In our hometown in east of J-province, there is an alternative: wearing light cyan shoes. This way, she could still mourn Daddy, but not too conspicuously.

Returning home at 16 East Dragon Lane, I noticed that there were a couple of other families lived in the first floor. Mama and my sister lived on the second floor in a small room, used to be the *Yangs'* study. In 1956, during the campaign called "Joint State-Private Ownership," Yang's wife, a middle school teacher, participated, and the house became joint property with the local government. They were allowed to have the second floor for their own use. The government would rent out the first floor and collect the rent.

Mama was glad to see me growing taller. She told me that with help from friends, she was able to find a job as a substitute teacher. She had a degree in education with years of teaching experience. However, by the time she returned to N-city in 1959, she had left the workplace for nearly 20 years. To be more competent as a teacher, she enrolled in the Night University of N-city. Near 50 years old, she attended the classes punctually, rain or shine.

---

[45]   Since 1954, a so-called "Resident Committee" has been organized in cities. Normally, one such a committee consists of 100 -700 families. Among its many functions is to report to the security department about anything they think is politically incorrect.

Due to bleach shortage in the early 1960s, the paper was coffee-colored. The textbooks were printed using such paper. It was not hard to imagine what efforts were required for her to read those textbooks. She finally completed all required courses and graduated in 1961. After that, she found a full-time job in an elementary school for 20 *Yuan* RMB a month. Since working full-time, Mama did not have time to cook lunch. She arranged my sister to eat at her school. I would go to Mama's school, and eat lunch together in a nearby public cafeteria.

One day, when I went to her school, she was still teaching music class. I saw her playing the organ and was surprised. I did not know Mama had this skill. After class, I excitingly asked her to play more. She played several songs of the 1930s, and told me that she learned piano and organ when attending *Jinan* University.

After returning to N-city, I went to a couple of the nearby high schools to see if there was a vacancy available for me to continue my study. Finally, the Third High of N-city accepted me. Due to my low family income, and I made good grades, the school gave me the Assistantship of 4 *Yuan* RMB a month, and waived my tuition.[46]

In the fall of 1960, I started my second year of high school. One of our courses was solid geometry. Our teacher was a lady who just graduated from the graduate school of the Beijing Teacher's University. We were glad that she had excellent academic credential. However, her class was not well organized. She did not follow the sequence of the textbook, and rarely wrote anything on the blackboard. We complained to the school leaders about this.

One afternoon, the dean of education came to our classroom to have a meeting with us. He said that this teacher had a Master's degree, and that she was from the best teacher's university in the nation. Some classmates rejected this by asking what was good about this, if we could not understand what she was teaching, and could not do our homework. The dean could not refute this argument. After thinking for a while, he told us that as the new semester had already started, all teachers had been assigned their tasks. Now only Mr. *Zou*, a young teacher, was available.

"Are you willing to let Mr. *Zou* try one lesson?" The dean asked.

---

46   In Mao's era, students in elementary and middle schools needed to pay tuitions.

Some students agreed with joy, and there was no objection because one more choice would not hurt. So, the dean decided to let Mr. *Zou* teach one lesson in the next class.

After the meeting, I asked those, who gladly accepted the dean's proposal, about Mr. *Zou*, and was told that he was graduated from this high school in the summer with excellent grades. However, due to his Landlord Class family background, he was not able to enter college. Appreciating his outstanding talent, the school offered him a teaching position, and he accepted. According to his former classmates, he was smart, and was the best student in the class. Now he was still doing the preparatory self-study, and had not been assigned any teaching task, so, he was available.

In the next class, Mr. *Zou* came to our classroom. He was so young that he looked just like one of us. However, he showed strong self-confidence, and started the lecture with clear and vibrant voice. Also, he wrote on the blackboard neatly, which made it easy for us to take notes. Apparently, he rehearsed the class many times, so when he just stopped talking, the end-class-bell started ringing. We were so glad that we all applauded spontaneously. As a result, the school decided to let Mr. *Zou* continue teaching our solid geometry until we finished this course.

In 1950s, "Sino-Soviet Friendship Association," a nationwide organization, was established, and every city had a branch. This association organized us to communicate with the students in the Soviet Union by mail. We initiated the activity by writing a draft letter in Russian, addressing to "Soviet Friends," and submitting to Mr. *Liu*, our Russian teacher, for reviewing, and editing. Mr. *Liu* used to be an English teacher. After the Liberation, he was sent to a language school for one year to study Russian, and then became a Russian teacher.

After his review, we would carefully copy the edited draft, and submit the final version to our school leaders. Then, the letters would be collected by the city branch of the Sino-Soviet Friendship Association, and be mailed to the Soviet Union. After the counterpart of the association in the Soviet Union received our letters, they would pair Soviet students with Chinese students on one-to-one basis. The individual student would reply to us by addressing to each of us directly with their names signed. Then we would exchange letters with the assigned Soviet students individually. Of course, the letter-writing process was the same as the first letter. Their replies were in Russian, rather than in Chinese, and the letters were mainly about their daily lives in their schools, and were very simple so that we could read them easily. The Soviet stamps were well-made, colorful, and highly sought by stamp collectors.

In the New Year of 1961, I received a letter, and a New Year Card from my Soviet friend. The card was a black and white photo of the cone shaped Sputnik 2 with "Happy New Year" in Russian. I was so glad that I carefully kept this card as my treasure.

However, that was the last letter I received from this Soviet student, after that the letter-exchange activity stopped without any formal announcement. A couple of years later, I learned that the Soviet Union was no longer regarded as the Big Brother of China, and the two communist parties started arguing publicly. The Communist Party of China published nine commentaries to criticize the Soviet Communist Party and denounced the Soviet Union as "the revisionist country," who betrayed Marx-Leninism. The SCP called the CPC the dogmatist.

Entering 1961, the shortage of food and other daily living supplies became quite severe. Various ration coupons, such as coupons for rice, cooking oil, sugar, soap, cloth, tofu and soybean products, bicycles, wrist watches, etc., were issued, and new kinds of ration coupons kept coming.

Since 1953, some areas have started issuing the ration coupon of food. In these areas people needed to have money as well as the food coupon to buy rice, wheat flour, millet, etc. starting in 1955, the food coupon was adopted nationwide. In addition to the nationwide food coupon, which could be used in any province, each province also issued the provisional food coupon, which could only be used within the specific province.

At the beginning when the food coupons were implemented, the food supply was sufficient. Most of the time, people would have some unused coupons left by the end of the month. People did not feel any shortage. However, since 1960, the newspaper and radio broadcast repeatedly told us that due to the natural disasters,[47] farmers could not produce enough food and cooking oil. As a result, the food coupon was reduced quite a

---

[47] Many years later, we learned that this was one of the consequences of the Big Leap Forward.

bit. The meat was also in short supply. We were told that this was because the revisionist Soviet Union wanted China to pay their military supplies during the Korean War with pigs. The ration coupons for cooking oil and many other daily necessities were issued.

Most of the time, we had to eat mixed rice-and-vegetable porridge, because buying vegetables did not require a coupon. The most widely used vegetables were cabbage and Daikon radish. Some vendors put a coal stove on the sidewalk to cook and sell such porridge, others would boil sweet potatoes for sale. Frequently, I saw groups of people using ladders to take the leaves of the trees along streets, and some other groups collecting the gum of some trees. Those materials were processed and added to the rice soup as supplements.

Since the cloth-coupon was also not enough, people demonstrated their ingenuity by making clothes for children using handkerchiefs, which did not require a cloth coupon to buy.

With the food ration, everybody felt hungry all the time. But Mama always shared part of her rice with my sister and me. We knew she was hungry as well, and did not want her rice. She would manage to make some burps to pretend to be full up. If we continued to decline, she would tell us that she'd be angry if we did not accept her offer. As a result, she lost a lot of weight. Once a relative visited us and was surprised to see that she had become so thin that he had barely recognized her.

Around that time, beggars appeared and were called *"Anhui* Guys" because most of them were from *Anhui* province.[48] They would wander in restaurants, standing beside the eating customers. Then beggars would suddenly put their dirty hands into the bowel or the plate. In such cases, customers would let those beggars pick up the remaining food to eat.

One day, when I went home for lunch, I saw a haggard teenage boy, like an eagle, swooping on a small girl and grabbing her *Man Tou* (a piece of steamed bread), and then running away. The girl cried helplessly.

On a rainy day, when I went to my school, I heard that a student in our junior high section had tried to steal a *Man Tou* from the school's cafeteria. He took a javelin in our physical education department, and tried to reach a *Man Tou* through the window. The noise alerted the patrol team, and he

[48] Anhui is another province with a quarter of its population perished due to the famine.

was caught. As a punishment, the school leaders organized all students to see the scene. Walking in a single line, we passed by this student. When approaching him, I saw the javelin, with the *Man Tou* pierced on its head, next to him. He was sobbing with lowered head.

To save energy, we stopped physical activities in our physical education class. The P.E. class was changed to "*Nei Tang* (physical education inside the classroom)." The P.E. teacher frequently described the food he had eaten when attending the College of Sports. Because of their intense training programs, the students there ate high energy food, such as beef, pork, eggs, milk, etc. We liked this, especially when he described the banquet in the Chinese New Year and holidays. He would bring some cookbooks with colored pictures to show many dishes that we had never heard of. Occasionally, some students would comment: "Ah, I wish the pictures were real!" The whole class would burst out laughing in such occasions.

Also, some high-end cookies, cakes, candies, cigarettes, and liquors, appeared in the shops. There was no ration coupon required to buy them, but they were several times more expensive than the ordinary counterparts, which did require coupons. It was said that there was too much cash in people's hands. This measure would facilitate the cash to be returned to the central bank.

A noticeable trend developed during that time. Several phrases: The Class, the Class Struggle, and the Class Line, were frequently mentioned in the broadcast, newspaper, and meetings. To us, the most relevant phrase was the Class Line. The main idea of the Class Line was to limit higher education opportunities for those who were from the families of the Exploitive Classes,[49] and those who had family members or relatives with political problems. We were required to fill the "Family Background Form," to report our family information. There were several columns in the form. The first was about the family members. Grandparents from the father's side, parents, brothers and sisters, married or not, were defined as the family members. Another column was the Social Relations, which included grandparents from the mother's side, uncles and aunts, etc. Also,

---

49   Exploitive Classes are Landlord, Rich Peasant, and Capitalist, which were determined in early 1950s.

there were two special columns. One of them was for reporting the family members or relatives who were prisoned, under surveillance, or executed. The other was for reporting family members or relatives who were overseas, including those in Taiwan, Hong Kong, and Macao.

My father was put into prison in 1958, I must report this in the former special column. We were told that if we hid any of such information and were discovered, the punishment would be severe.

It was not hard to image that each time when filling this kind of form, I was very stressful. Especially, I was worried after hearing that students, who were from the families with various political problems, would have hard time to pass the family's political background check for the higher education. Without passing this check, those students would be disqualified to attend colleges, no matter how well they would do in their study, and in the national college entrance examination. Mr. *Zou*, who taught us Solid Geometry, was one of them.

When entering the third school year in the fall of 1961, I heard another bad news, Mr. *Huang*, who had just graduated in summer, could not attend college because of his Landlord family background. Again, since his excellent academic achievements, he was hired by our school to teach physics. This made me more worried about my future.

Our high school had been the number one in the nationwide college entrance examination in J-province since 1958. The school indeed had some special arrangement. First, all the teachers, teaching the classes for the students in their third, i.e. the last school year, were the best in the school. Secondly, the curriculum for the third school year was so arranged that all required courses would end in March, rather than in June. This would have three extra months for the student to prepare for the entrance examination. Thirdly, the classes were rearranged based on the students' future plans. Those, who wanted to study science and engineering, would be in one class. Those, who decided to study medicine and agriculture, would be rearranged into another class. Those, who wanted to study literature, arts, and history, were organized into yet another class. The review materials for the three classes would be different because the test papers for the three categories were different. Finally, a rally was held before the preparation stage started: a prominent alumnus would be invited to give a speech to the students.

In 1962, an alumnus, who had studied in the University of Moscow, was to give us such a speech. He wore a brown suit[50] and a bright green tie, which was quite unusual at that time. He was eloquent and humorous, with the body language we saw in the Soviet Movies. He told us how hard they studied in the Soviet Union, and got high grades. He also singed a Soviet song in Russian. Finally, he encouraged us to study hard and wished us well in the upcoming entrance examination. We all listened to him attentively, and showed enormous admiration. After this rally, we were all excited, and determined to do our best to get top grades in our entrance examination.

Our preparation was divided into three stages. The first stage was to review systematically. Our teachers complied our reviewing materials, mimeographed them, and distributed to us. After the first stage, we would take an exam. Based on the results, the teachers would go over the areas that we did not do well in the exam. In the final stage, the teachers would go over the areas they thought were the most important and likely to be in the real test paper.

The nationwide college entrance examination was, and still is the largest examination in China. It is held once a year on the same days nationwide, and the test paper is the top state secret. Our test papers were airlifted to the test locations, one day before the examination and was guarded by the armed PLA soldiers. Several different sets of test paper were prepared. In case one set was leaked, the alternative set would be used.

It was said that the atmosphere was so stressful that some students fainted upon entering the test room. To better prepare students, our school organized several simulated entrance exams. Each would be one step closer to the real one. The first step was to let us take the exams in different classrooms, then we were given simulated examination IDs with our photos. In the last stage, we were given the exam papers, which were like the real ones with a corner folded. We were not allowed to open the fold corner, and would not put our names on them, because all the relevant information was in the folded corner.

Near the end of 1961, our school announced some documents from the central government, which said that Chiang Kai-Shek could attack

---

[50]   After the Liberation, rarely any one would wear the western suit. Only after 1978, did people wear the suit again.

the mainland. Organizations, including our school, prepared emergency shelters for possible air raids by Chiang's air force. We were told that in case when the air raid happened during the entrance examination, the teacher, who was monitoring the test room, would lead students to the specified shelter. We would not be allowed to bring anything from the test room, nor would we be allowed to speak to each other, to avoid possible cheating.

Since Chiang might use airborne soldiers, and they could pretend to be the PLA soldiers, some materials were distributed to teach people how to distinguish the true and false PLA soldiers. For example, the PLA soldiers would call each other "comrade", Chiang's soldiers would call each other "brothers;" the PLA soldiers would also call civilians "comrade," Chiang's soldiers would call civilians "uncle, aunt, brother, sister," etc., based on age and sex. Some photos in those materials were included to show the differences between the shoe prints of true and false PLA soldiers. Once the false PLA soldiers were discovered, people should report to the local public security department immediately.

Finally, the real examination came. We were told that the school would provide everyone with a free breakfast. When we went to the school for the breakfast, some student volunteers would remind us whether we brought our examination IDs. Without the ID, one would not be allowed to enter the test room. If anyone forgot, they would still have time to go home and take it.

Owning to the simulated exams, we felt quite at home when entering the true examination rooms. There was no air raid by Chiang Kai-Shek, nor was there anybody fainted. The examination went smoothly. After the examination, we reviewed our answers with our teachers so that we could estimate our scores. On the whole, I did quite well in this big examination, and felt great relief.

A few days of relief quickly replaced by anxiously waiting. Our application form had two columns. Each column had twelve choices. The first column was to fill the names of so-called "key universities." There were eighty key universities, which were directly managed by the Ministry of Education. These universities were better equipped, and had the top-rated professors. Being a radio amateur, I naturally wanted to pursue a career in this area. But this specialty was closely related to the national defense, my family background would hinder me. So, my first choice was the Department of Electrical Engineering at Tsinghua University. The remaining choices in this column were not critical, because a key university had rarely admitted an applicant who did not put this key university as the first choice.

The second column was for other universities, mainly the provincial universities, which were managed by the provincial government. At that time in N-city, there were three provincial universities that provide science and engineering programs with total 9 departments. I filled the first 9 choices with the 9 departments. Then I filled the 10th choice with the Department of Mechanical and Electrical Engineering at the J-Institute of Metallurgy, located in G-city, and left the last two choices blank because there was no other department that I was interested in.

With my excellent academic performance, I thought I could attend Tsinghua University. Nevertheless, I was not quite sure how my father's problem would affect me.

The acceptance letters were finally sent out in two batches. The first batch was sent to those who were admitted by key universities. I did not receive anything in the first batch. I came to realize that the family background had played an important role,[51] and was depressed. For a couple of days, I could not fall asleep, watching the sky, staring at the stars, until dawn.

Mr. *Tu*, my classmate and a good friend, was also an excellent student. He was selected to represent our school to participate in a mathematics competition in N-city, and was awarded for his performance. We shared many common interests, such as playing *erhu*, a two-string music instrument, and playing Chinese chess.

One evening, after a visit to my home, I walked him to his home and saw Mr. *Luo*, our Teacher-in-Charge. After greeting, we asked him whether he heard any news regarding the second batch of acceptance letters. Mr. *Luo* told us that I might be accepted by the Department of Physics in the J-province University. But Mr. *Tu* might have been rejected because he

---

51   Later I learned that in 1961, several central leaders, including Premier *Zhou Enlai*, emphasized that a student's academic performance was as important as a soldier's military skills. So, when admitting students, standard for family background check was loosed. This was why I was accepted by a college. Otherwise, I might have been rejected.

did not see Mr. *Tu*'s name in the list of admitted students. Mr. *Tu*'s father escaped to Hong Kong in the early 1950s, so he had "oversea relationship." Mr. *Luo* believed this was too serious to pass the family background check.

Upon hearing this, Mr. *Tu* could not stand steadily and almost fainted. I quickly hold his shoulder, and found him sweating so badly that his T-shirt was quickly soaked. Mr. *Luo* fell into silence, showing great compassion. I walked Mr. *Tu* to his home. Upon hearing the bad news, the mother and son embraced each other and broke into tears.

Later, our school also offered him a teaching position, but he turned it down, and went to work in a textile factory, because he wanted to be a member of the Working Class, or Proletarian Class. This way, his children would have a better family background.

When receiving my acceptance letter, I found it was not from the Department of Physics at the J-province University, but from the J-Institute of Metallurgy, my last choice in the second column. I was not very happy with this college, but Mama was elated. She told me that based on her own experience, unlike many people believed, the fame of a university would not play big a role in a student's future. She said that many eminent people, such as Michael Faraday, did not even have a college degree. Her words encourage me, and also boosted my spirit.

G-city (1962-1968)

At the end of August of 1962, I left for G-city by long distance bus. About a dozen passengers were admitted to the same college as mine and traveled with me. After two days, we arrived at G-city station in the late afternoon. Each of us used a *Biandan*, or a carrying-pole, to carry the baggage, and walked to our college. Some student volunteers had set up a station to welcome new students. After showing our acceptance letters, we were brought to our assigned dormitories, respectively. During Mao's era, there was no tuition for all college students, and all college students lived in the dormitories on campus, free of charge. In addition, all college students had free medical care.

The J-Institute of Metallurgy used to be a provincial technical school. In the Big Leap Forward of 1958, it was upgraded to a college and was taken over by the Ministry of Metallurgy in 1962. In Mao's era, the number of students admitted each year and for each specialty were based on the Five-Year Plan developed by the Central Planning Committee. Nearly all colleges required five years of study (Beijing University and Tsinghua University required six years of schooling, and some teacher's universities were of four year).

When I attended this college, there were two departments: The Department of Mining and Mineral Processing which had two specialties: Mining and Mineral Processing. The other was the Department of Mechanical and Electrical Engineering, which also had two specialties: Metallurgical Machinery and Electrical and Mechanical Mining Equipment. Like the elementary and middle schools, the basic unit in Colleges was also the class. Each specialty had one or more classes based on the number of students admitted. Each class would admit 30 students. Like the high school, each class in college also had student monitors to handle various class-related affairs, and a branch of the Communist Youth League, which was headed by a secretary, a head for Organization, which was responsible for accepting new members, and a head for Propaganda.

My class admitted 30 students, but only 26 actually enrolled, with two females. A year later, one classmate dropped out, and only 25 continued studying until the graduation.

The college had three campuses. The main campus was quite large with three small lakes. The main gate was on the west side of the campus facing an east-west boulevard. There was a small garden inside the main gate. In the north of the garden, there was a two-story gray cement building, the building of the Department of Mining and Mineral Processing. The building for our department was of red-brick with three stories. Our classroom was on the second floor. Unlike most Western universities, where the students would take different courses in different classrooms, in our college, professors would come to our classroom for various courses. In addition, we had several other buildings for the administration, the library, labs, etc. There was a gymnasium, a sports field with a soccer field, many basketball courts, and an auditorium, which also served as a theater. There were two dining halls, one for students, and one for faculty members and other college workers. Student's dormitories were also on the campus, and our dormitory was on the east side. All female students lived together in a separate dormitory.

Our college also had an attached manufacturing factory, with machine tools, casting, forging, and welding plants for student to practice. The houses for faculty members and other workers and a medical clinic were in two separate campuses not far from the main campus.

In the first year, dancing parties were held in the auditorium in Saturday evenings. Students would take turns to move the long benches along the walls so that the center part could be used for dancing. Students would learn dancing in the third year when they were about to do their course-related engineering practice in factories or mining companies. During these practices, parties would be held so that the students would dance with workers. The purpose of the parties was to make good relationship between the students and the workers.

However, dancing was regarded as the bourgeoisie life style, and banned in China in 1963.[52]

---

[52] The ban was lifted in 1980s after the Cultural Revolution.

All colleges provided financial aid to students based on the family financial conditions of students. There were four levels. Level A with a monthly stipend of 16 *Yuan* RMB was for the orphan student. Level B, 14 *Yuan*, and Level C, 10 *Yuan*, and Level D 8 *Yuan*. I was given Level B Aid due to my family's difficult financial condition. We need to pay 10 *Yuan* a month to the student dining hall. Mother would send me 3 *Yuan* a month as an allowance. So, I had 7 *Yuan* in total, for other expenses, such as textbooks, stationeries, and movie tickets, etc. It was far from enough. So, I had to work in the winter and summer vacations to earn additional money.

Normally the school would provide us with such opportunities. At first, we did physical labor, such as working on various construction projects. Starting in the summer of 1964, I worked on plotting educational diagrams for our courses, using the engineering drawing technique we learned in our Engineering drawing class. Naturally, the wages were higher than that of the physical labor.

In addition to the technical courses, we also had physical education for the first two years. Due to the big famine, and the tuberculosis I suffered during my high school years, I became very weak. This caused difficulties in my PE class. To catch up with my classmates, I started jogging each morning and went to the gymnasium in the afternoon for one-hour workout. My efforts did bear fruits. During the second semester, I earned an A in PE. The professor told me that based on my actual performance, I was not yet qualified for the A. However, considering the good progress I had made since the last semester, I deserve this good grade as an encouragement.

The food shortage also affected our meal schedule: the student dining hall offered two meals on Sundays because there was no class. After the noon nap in Sundays, we normally would stay in bed to read books, and waiting for the school's wired broadcast to signal the time for the second meal. Watches were very expensive, most of my classmates could not afford it.

One Sunday in November, upon hearing the wired broadcast, we got up and went to the student dining hall. We happened to have *Hongshao Rou* (Chinese roasted pork) for dinner. Since childhood, I did not like the fatty roast pork. But that Sunday, I found the fatty pork especially aromatic. I tried one piece, and for the first time in my life, I felt the fatty pork was so delicious.

I could not afford the long-distance bus ticket and stayed on campus during the first winter vacation, and was the first time in my life to spend the 1963 Chinese New Year away from my family. Besides, I also need to use the winter vacation to earn additional money. Like me, more than a half of my classmates could not afford the two-way bus tickets and stayed. The college leaders kindly managed to buy some cookies and fruits for us to celebrate this traditional holiday.

Entering 1963, although the food and other supplies improved a little bit, we still felt hungry all the time. Some classmates suspected that they might have been infected with roundworms. Because the roundworm took away some of nutrients, they believed this was why they had been feeling hungry all the time. They went to our school's clinic to ask for the ascarcide. After taking the medicine, a couple of my classmates indeed had their roundworms expelled out. I followed suit. But I did not see any roundworm. Suspecting that the dosage might not be enough, I asked the doctor to give me stronger dosage. The doctor explained that if no roundworm was seen, then I was not infected. Increasing dosage could hurt my liver.

After that, I turned to the newspapers and magazines for health and nutrition related information. One day, I came across an article saying that the nutrition of one ounce of soybean sauce was about the same as that of one egg. That was good news because it required ration coupon to buy eggs, but buying soybean sauce did not require any coupon. So, I bought soybean sauce and mixed it with water to make soups. This made me a laughing stock for a while.

In the meantime, we started to explore food that was available without requiring any ration coupon. We visited the nearby villages and found that local farmers were selling sweet potatoes and water chestnuts, both required no coupon to buy. So we bought woks, used three bricks to make a stove, and collected offcuts from the school's carpenter's plant. From then on, cooking sweet potatoes and water chestnut became one of our favorite entertainments on Sundays.

In the spring of 1963, Mr. *Hu*,[53] a professor of the Middle-South Institute of Mining and Metallurgy, and an expert in mineral processing, was

---

[53] In 1957, Mr. *Hu* was labeled as the rightist. But he was rehabilitated around 1960. Because of this, the president was denounced, during the Cultural Revolution, for letting a "de-capped" rightist to poison young students' thought.

invited by the president of our college to give academic lectures for the Department of Mining and Mineral processing.

At the end, he was also invited to give a speech to all students. His speech was "If I would have attended a college again." According to his speech, he graduated from *Jiao tong* University in Shanghai in 1945, and obtained a Master's degree from the University of Utah in 1948. He was eloquent, humorous, had a broad spectrum of knowledge, and frequently quoting classical Chinese poems. In the speech, he used his life experience to make points. For example, his parents were not rich, and he could not afford the drawing instruments when attending the college. So, he had to borrow, from the neighboring students, the instruments which were not in use at that moment, to draw his homework. However, the financial hardship did not hinder him. He graduated with excellent grades, and continued his study in the United States. His experience greatly inspired me.

Starting in the early 1950s, bookstores were my favorite places to visit. One day when I visited a local branch of *Xinhua* Bookstore, I saw a newly published book, "Minimum Russian Vocabulary" by the Foreign Language Dept. of Tsinghua University. In the preface, it said that they used the statistic method to analyze a huge collection of Russian science and engineering literature, and selected 3000 words that had the highest frequency of appearance. The group believed that after memorizing the 3000 words, the students would have less than 5 percent chance to encounter unknown words, when reading Russian technical literatures. I was excited, and bought a copy immediately.

During the summer vacation, I made some flashcards with the words in this book, and learned the words that I had not yet known. After that I was able to read Russian mathematic textbooks. With additional efforts, I started reading Russian engineering magazines, and got some advanced technological news from them. I was quite proud of that.

Since the Big Leap Forward campaign, the relationship between *"Hong"*[54] and *"Zhuan"* (Red and Expertise) had been raised and discussed. *"Zhuan"*

---

[54]   *Hong*, literally means red color, but figuratively means politically correct by the standard of the Chinese communist party. *"Bai"* or white was the opposite, and means politically incorrect.

or Expertise, was relatively easy to define and understand. But "Red" was impalpable. In the "Guidelines about Higher Education (draft)," there was some explanation: "For the professors and students in the institution of higher education, the Red should be embodied not only in ideology, but also in their teaching and learning practice... Only those insisted on opposing the leadership of the communist party, and opposing socialism could be called 'White.' Calling those, who were good at their daily work, but politically inactive or neutral, to be 'white with expertise' is incorrect."

However, in early 1963, the debate started again. Somebody proposed that "The contradiction between Red and Expertise is the contradiction between the proletarian ideology and capitalist ideology, is the contradiction between the socialist road and capitalist road. The way to resolve the contradiction is to promote the proletarian ideology and crack down the capitalist ideology." This made the topic more confusing. As a result, even some high-ranking officers explained "red" differently, and no clear and definite conclusion was reached. Nevertheless, those who made good grades in their studies were often labeled as "*Zhi Zhuan, by Hong* (biased toward expertise, but not red)." This label was in my yearly review in all my college years. So, I had never been admitted to the Communist Youth League.

On March 3, 1963 Chairman Mao called on to learn from Mr. *Lei Feng*, the PLA soldier who died in an accident at age of 22. The propaganda apparatus started publishing articles, poems, and songs, etc. to promote *Lei Feng*. His diary was also published. In 1958, "Beijing Daily" published an editorial which conveyed a speech by Mr. *Liu Shaoqi*, who would become the president of the People's Republic of China in 1959, calling on becoming "the Party's tame tool." This editorial later published offprint for wide distribution. In his diary of October 11, 1958, *Le Feng* wrote: "I would strengthen my self-discipline, carefully study the constitution of the Chinese Communist Youth League and related books, follow the instructions of the Party, resolutely and unconditionally be a tame tool of the Party." It was apparent that *Lei Feng* had learned *Liu*'s words, and used them in his diary. Due to the propaganda, whether one was willing to be a tame tool of the Party became an ultimate standard of "Red." To be a "revolutionary screw," as *Lei Feng* expressed in his diary, was a popular phrase in those days.

In addition, one of *Le Feng*'s poem was also frequently quoted:

Treating comrades should be as warm as spring,
Doing work should be as enthusiastic as summer,
Overcoming individualism[55] should be like the wind
whipping off the leaves in fall,
Handling enemies should be as cruel as winter.

After setting *Lei Feng* as a model, Chairman Mao called for the whole nation to learn from the People's Liberation Army in 1964. A new nationwide "learning from the PLA" campaign started. Similar to the political commissar in the PLA, our college assigned a political advisor for each class for ideological education.

The Political Department of the PLA compiled and printed the famous little red book, Chairman Mao's Quotation, and distributed to every soldier. In the meantime, the fourth volume of Mao's Selected Works was published. To respond to Chairman Mao's call, everyone in my class bought a copy of the Volume 4 and started reading. Several times a week, meetings were held to discuss some articles in this volume.

This year, the government issued "Three Disciplines" for college students:

1. One must obey the job assignment of the government.
2. Student marriage is strictly forbidden.
3. Romance is no allowed.

The first discipline was only required when the students graduated and the job assignments took place.[56] The second issue was the result of student romance. So, one of the political advisor's tasks was to monitor the possible romance activities among students.

After the Three Disciplines were announced, no student would openly

---

55 In China, individualism is regarded as a shortcoming, collectivism is advocated by the Party.
56 Upon graduation, all college students were assigned jobs based on the Five-Year plan.

show his or her romance. The love activities went underground. Saturday evening was the most likely romantic time. Therefore, political advisors had to hide and stay in the places where lovers would be likely to stay. These efforts appeared not in vein. Frequently our political advisor would organize meetings, and told us that he had discovered some underground romance activities. He even quoted some students' alleged romantic words, and warned that for now he would not point out the names of these students. If they were caught again, he would openly discipline them. Until our graduation, nobody in my class was disciplined.

However, this strict regulation was not foolproof. Miss *Chu*, who entered the college in 1960, had sex with many male students. She liked to write down all the events in her diary, with details about the time, location, male students' names, etc., in each such case. This diary was discovered by her roommates and handed over to the college leaders. As a result, she was expelled from the college. With her detailed diary, all involved male students were also punished, ranging from expelling from the Communist Youth League, to depriving of the leadership positions in the student union.

After China and Soviet Union openly broke up, China was surrounded by imperialist, revisionists, and counter-revolutionary countries and groups. To cope with such a situation, and also as a part of learning from the PLA, the central government decided to establish a militia. Every unit set up a specific department, normally headed by a PLA veteran, to organize the military training. We had lectures on using and maintaining rifles. Finally, everyone was given five bullets for practice in the last day of the training. However, like the "every-citizen-is-a-soldier" campaign in 1958, this military training was not on a regular basis.

March 12, 1964, *Guangming* Daily, an intellectual-oriented Chinese newspaper, published the commentary "*Rang Qingchun Fangchu guanghui!* (Let our youth be brilliant)." In the article, the author briefly introduced scientists from Galileo Galilei to Albert Einstein, litterateurs from Aleksandr Pushkin to Maxim Gorky, and revolutionists from Karl Marx to Chairman Mao. All of them made great achievement when they were young. This article was like a stone thrown into a lake that caused big waves among the young college students. Everyone was inspired, excited, and wanted their youth to be as brilliant as those mentioned in the article.

However, this commentary was soon criticized. For example, "*Zhongguo Qingnian* (Chinese Youth)" magazine publish an article argued: "*Lei Feng* lived only for 22 years, he did not have any invention, nor did he publish any scientific paper or book. He was just an ordinary soldier. But he aimed high and 'dedicated his youth to the greatest cause of the world – to liberate mankind.'[57] *Lei Feng's* short life is indeed a great and brilliant life."

Although the original commentary did mention the greatest revolutionary leaders, such as Marx, Engels, Lenin, Stalin, and Chairman Mao, it seemed that "Chinese Youth" magazine did not like the mentioning of those young Western scientists and litterateurs, whom *Lei Feng* was compared with. *Guangming* Daily did not publish any following article to defend. As a result, the enthusiasm stimulated by the commentary lost steam. I was totally perplexed as to why a youth-oriented magazine would be so irritated by the commentary that encouraged young people to become great scientists and litterateurs? Didn't China need eminent scientists and litterateurs? With only "revolutionary screws," how could we build a machine? However, already being criticized as "biased toward expertise, but not red," I did not want to invite more trouble by raising such questions.

Oct. 16, 1964, we all were excited about the news that China had successfully tested its first atomic bomb. From a young age, we all learned in our history and political classes that since 19th century China had suffered many humiliating defeats by foreigners, notably the defeat by British Empire in the 1840 Opium war, the defeat by Japan in1894 Sino-Japanese War, and the defeat by Eight-Nation Alliance in 1900, which caused the Beijing's spectacular royal garden *Yuanmingyuan* to be destroyed. More than one hundred years of humiliation caused everyone to be proud of this great achievement. Students celebrated this event with a parade on our campuses.

In the following days, the newspaper published a large number of photos of the mushroom cloud, poems praising this great achievement, and some article to describe the research and development process. Soon, the newsreel about the first atomic bomb was released. We were organized to watch it.

---

57   This quote is from the novel "How is the steel made?" by Soviet novelist Nikolai Ostrovsky

Coincidentally, Nikita Khrushchev was ousted on the same day. Since Khrushchev was accused by the official media as the Soviet leader who caused the rift between the two communist parties, for a short time, we expected that the relationship between the two countries would improve. But later we found that the relationship between the two countries just kept getting worse.

In 1964, there was another political campaign under way. It was called "Socialist Education," which was also called "*Si Qing*" or Four Cleanups: Cleanup Work Points,[58] accounts, warehouses, and properties of People's communes. Later, the Four Cleanups were updated to clean up politics, economy, organizations, and ideology. College students were required to participate.

Our college leaders arranged the fall semester to end about one month earlier in the middle of December. After that we studied the campaign guidelines called "*Shuang Shi Tiao* (twin Ten Articles) and other related documents, issued by the central government. We were also organized to listen to the recorded speech by Comrade *Dong Pu*. She started a pilot "*Si Qing*" project in *Taoyuan* production team in *Hebei* province. In her speech, she conveyed then President *Liu Shaoqi's* opinion that "Peaceful evolution[59] have already taken place in our higher leadership. The leaders in provinces and cities had already had their[60] representatives," etc.

The key points in her speech were that when we entered the people's commune, we needed to test the water, visit the Poor and Lower-Middle peasants first, to determine who would be trustworthy. Then we would mobilize those trusted people to expose those who were problematic. Then the problematic officers would be replaced by the reliable Poor and Lower-Middle peasants.

Later, we learned that Comrade *Dong Pu* was *Wang Guangmei*, the wife of President *Liu Shaoqi*.

---

[58] A system in the People's Commune to record the farmers' daily work in the commune.

[59] In China, the phrase "Peaceful Evolution" means the society gradually changed from communist, or "socialist," as was officially called by the government, to capitalist.

[60] Here "they" implies the class enemies in general.

We were arranged to go to *Shazhouba* People's Commune in *Ruijin* County. *Ruijin* was also called *"Hong Du* (Red Capital) because on November 7, 1931, the Chinese Communist Party established the Soviet Republic of China there.

After the New Year's Day of 1965, several trucks brought us to *Shazhouba* People's Commune, and we were divided into smaller groups to live in the peasants' homes. I lived together with several students from other classes, in a big house, which had a gate and a big courtyard. The dialect of *Ruijin* area was quite different. Not only did the local people pronounce the words differently, but also, they name things differently. On the other hand, since the broadcast and movies were in Mandarin, they could understand us. It took me a while to get used to their dialect, and to be able to communicate with the local peasants.

Frequently we joined the peasants to work in the field. During working, we also chatted with them. At first, some of the low-ranking cadre would approach us to chat. They had better education, and could speak Mandarin. Probably they wanted to get some information of this campaign from us. However, we were afraid that those officers could be the target of the *Si Qing* campaign. To be associated with such problematic people would be a serious politic mistake. Therefore, we normally just politely greeted them with a smile, and then would find some excuse to walk away. After several such incidents they realized that we were not willing to talk to them. So, they no longer came to bother us.

There already had been a *Si Qing* Working Group there. They were officers from different units, and were the main force of this campaign. Our task was to assist them, and in the meantime to learn the proletarian ideology from the Poor and Lower-Middle peasants. What we did most was to help the Working Group in checking accounts of the production team. At first, our leaders planned to let us *"San Tong* (live, eat, and work together)" with the Poor and Lower-Middle peasants. But, for some reasons, the leaders changed their plan. A dining room was set up for all students lived in the same production team, which was a village.

In this village, I noticed that there were many dark green lumps on the walls of the peasants' houses. I asked the peasants what they were, and was told that these were wrapped leaves and vines of sweet potatoes. After dried, they were stored as food supplements to make porridge with rice.

After paying agricultural tax, they would have not enough rice to eat, so they need this stuff. I was surprised. At first, I thought the lumps were cow shit dried to be used as a fuel. *Shazhouba* was the old Red Base in 1930s. Now 16 years had passed since the Liberation, why people here were still so poor. Their houses were shabby, and looked lack of proper maintenance. Their clothes were tattered with many patches. One day, a leader of the *Si Qing* Working Group criticized the peasants:

"You are too lazy! This is why you eat porridge, and wear shabby clothes!"

Not far from the place we lived, there was a new house. A newly married young couple lived there. One day, when working with the peasants, I got a chance to chat with the young couple. The young man was born to a family of the Rich Peasant class in this village. Since the Rich Peasant class was regarded as "black," no girl from the families of the Poor or Lower-Middle Peasant classes, i.e. the red families, would want to marry him. Anxious, the young man's parents searched nearby villages, and found a family of the Landlord class. This family also had a son, looking for a wife. The family of Landlord class had an unmarried daughter, and the young man from the Rich Peasant class happened to have an unmarried sister. So, the young man's parents proposed that the two families trade their daughters so that both young men would have wives. The proposal was accepted and a deal was made!

Would such a marriage deal have love? Such a question was too private to ask. However, once when we sat under a bit tree for a rest during a break, I noticed the wife sat next to her husband, and used her handkerchief to wipe out the sweat on his face, affectionately. It seemed that this young couple did have love.

For thousands of years, farmers used manure as the fertilizer. Collecting manure was an important agricultural work. In *Ruijin* this activity was called "pick up dog's shit." To educate us ideologically, our leaders arranged us to pick-up dog's shit. We were asked not to be afraid of losing face, not to be afraid of the stink smell, and to work like the Poor and Low-Middle peasants. We would use a carrying-pole to carry two baskets, hold a shit-picking fork, and walk to the downtown of *Ruijin*. There was not much dog's shit on the road because few people lived on both sides of the road.

Although after the Liberation, it was forbidden to keep dogs in big cities, in smaller cities and towns like *Ruijin*, the residents were still allowed to keep dogs.

After entering the town, I did see more dog shits. We had to pick-up two full baskets of dog shits before going home. At first, I just picked up the dog's shit only. It would take me a whole day to accomplish such a task. Later I learned that the pig's shit was accepted as well. There were many families raised pigs in *Ruijin*. By cleaning up two to three pig sties, we could quickly fill up our baskets.

Soon, the residents heard that many college students, participating in the *Si Qing* campaign, would come to downtown picking up the dog shit. Several times the residents would approach me, and invited me to their houses to clean up their pig sties. In such cases, I could quickly complete my work and return home early.

After the Chinese New Year, the central government issued new guidelines for the *Si Qing* campaign. It was simply called "*Er Shi San Tiao* (Twenty Three Articles)," for short. In this document, the phrase "Capitalist Roader" was initially used. However, the document did not give any definition for it. When studying this document, people spent a lot of time discussing the possible meaning of this new phrase. Finally, most people agreed that the problematic officers in this campaign were the Capitalist Roaders.

One day when we returned from work, I saw the old lady living in this compound steaming rice with a big wood barrel. Thinking she might have some big party, I asked her how many guests she would have. She said she was not cooking for a big party, but for making the rice wine[61] for the water-buffaloes of their production team.

"Spring is coming. Water Buffaloes will work very hard to plow the field. They need to eat better," she said.

The food was still in short supply at that time. It seemed that the villagers understood what had a higher priority. She was illiterate, like many old women in the countryside. The knowledge was likely handed down by mouth from one generation to the next.

As a part of ideological education, we participated in the volunteer

---

[61] The rice wine is made of the sweet rice with some special yeast. It is very nutritious.

work to help so-called "*Wu Bao Hu* (family of Five Guarantees[62])," such as carrying drinking water, going to the nearby mountains to collect firewood, etc.

Another activity was to visit the important revolutionary sites, such as the Monument for the martyrs of Red Army soldiers, the building of the Central Government of Workers and Peasants, established by the Party in 1930s. We also listened to the stories told by old Red Army soldiers about the time they spent with Chairman Mao and other central leaders.

The most impressive was the visit to the *Ruijin* Memorial Hall of Martyrs. There were several exhibition halls. In the halls, the floor-to-ceiling cabinets with glass doors were placed along the walls. Inside the cabinets were thread-binding books with blue-gray colored covers. In the center area of the hall, there were some display cabinets with some books opened for viewing. I stopped at one such a cabinet and watched through its top glass. These books were like old-fashioned account books written vertically. Each line listed one martyr's name, his birthplace, age, military rank, and death place and time. The open books I saw were all the martyrs died in the battle in *Jinzhou* city of North-East of China in 1948. The highest ranked one on this open page was a colonel. I looked around the cabinets along the walls full of such books, a thrill of sorrow ran down my spine. It is not hard to imagine how fierce the battles were during the civil war. These martyrs left their homes and survived the Long March and the World War II, but were unable to see their loved ones again. In the exhibition hall, a background music was played lightly. It was a song in the local folk music style. One section of the lyrics was as follows:

...

See off my husband to join the Red Army,
Don't worry about our family,
I would take care of everything,
Oh, my husband, my dear husband!

...

---

[62] Those families are consisted of old couples who have lost the working capabilities and do not have children. The people's commune was to guarantee their five basic needs: food, clothes, housing, medical needs, and burials.

Near the exit of this hall, there was an oil painting describing a young lady seeing off her husband. Wearing gray colored Red Army uniform, carrying a rifle on his right shoulder, and walking towards a team of soldiers, the husband was looking back, and waving goodbye to his young wife. Did such couples realize that they could never see each other again? Could such a young man's name be listed in one of the blue-gray books? At this moment, I felt the lyrics "Oh, my husband, my dear husband" sounded especially heartbroken.

In early April, we finished our participation in the *Si Qing* campaign, and returned to our college for the spring semester. Since the leaders managed to make use of the winter vacation, we only lost about two months of studying time. So, we were still able to complete the required courses for the spring semester.

At the beginning of the fall semester in September, we were to go to W-city Iron and Steel Corp for our initial engineering practice, designed to let us become familiar with our future working environment. The college gave us the money for our travel in advance, so that the students could return home on the way to W-city. We were to meet near the end of August in N-city, and then we would go to W-city together. This arrangement saved my money to buy the ticket from G-city to N-city.

I had not seen Mama since 1962, when I left home to attend the college. Mama was very excited to see me after three long years. She told me that due to her low salary, she and my sister frequently worked on Sundays helping vegetable vendors to peel pea pods to earn some additional money. Learning they worked so hard, I was deeply moved.

After 1962, the Class Line became more and more restrictive to those whose family background was "exploitive classes," or had problematic family members or relatives. The background checks used to be performed by schools. But since 1964, the political background check was performed by both educational organizations and the public security departments jointly. My father's arrest became increasingly a negative factor.

In the summer of 1965, my sister graduated from junior high school. Her school recommended that she apply for a vocational school rather than a senior high school, because there was no chance for her to pass the family's political background check for higher education. Moreover, a graduate from a vocational school would be assigned a job by the local government, but a high school graduate would have no such a benefit, and had to find jobs by themselves. Although my sister wanted to become a doctor, she eventually applied a vocational school after discussing the situation with Mama and me. Owning to her good grades, she was admitted to the N-city Vocational School with the specialty in processing the Chinese Herbal Medicine.

In the same summer, my younger brother graduated from the well-known Beijing 101 Middle School. When filling the application form, he wrote letters to discuss it with me. The Class Line had become more and more restrictive, and in 1964 no student from the black families was admitted in our college. Based on this situation, I advised him to apply for the Beijing Institute of Iron and Steel.

Our younger uncle was the chairman of the Department of Metallurgy of the institute. He studied metallurgy at the University of Minnesota and received a PhD there. Upon graduation, he returned, in response to the call by the government to build the new China. He was assigned to teach in the Department of Metallurgy at the newly founded institute, which was built with the help from the Soviet Union. Due to his many contributions in making some special steel alloys, he was elected as the representative of the People's Congress of Beijing, and then the representative of the National People's Congress of China in 1964. The 101 high school leaders, the local public security department, and the admission office of the institute would certainly know that my brother had lived with this uncle since 1958. As a well-known expert in alloys, and a politically prestigious representative of the National People's Congress, this uncle's reputation could reduce Father's negative factor, and increase the chance to pass the background check. He was a straight-A student in such a prestigious high school, Naturally, he wanted to attend Tsinghua University. Nevertheless, after evaluating the situation, he accepted my suggestion and put the Beijing Institute of Iron and Steel as his first choice.

After the nationwide entrance examination, he wrote to me saying that he took off the day just before the entrance examination to have a good rest. He believed if one did not do well during the years in school, one day would not help. It was better to have a good rest and enter the examination room with a fresh brain. Sure enough, he did very well in the nationwide entrance examination.

Near the end of August, my brother sent a letter to us. I thought it must have been good news, so I handed it to Mama to let her know first. Mama opened the letter eagerly. But before finishing, she broke into tears. I was astonished and took over the letter. My brother was rejected![63] I could not believe what was on the paper. What I felt was just like my brother described in his letter:

"When reading this rejection letter, I thought it must be a nightmare. When I wake up in the morning, I would receive an acceptance letter from the Beijing Institute of Iron and Steel."

However, it was real. In August, N-city frequently had thunderstorms in the late afternoon. That was what happened that day. The roaring thunders and pouring rains perfectly reflected our feeling at that time.

In early September, we arrived at the W-city Steel Corp. This steel Corp was built in the first five-year plan, with the help from the Soviet Union. We were arranged to live in the dormitory which was located near the production areas.

First, a worker in the safety department of the company gave us a lecture about safety regulations in the production area. He introduced the safety rules, and emphasized the importance of wearing the protective gears. Then he told us some terrible stories about the past accidents which caused death and injuries. Some of the stories did not sound real, but would illustrate his points.

Before entering the production areas, each of us was given a notebook called "Confidential Notebook" with numbers printed on each page. During the practice, we must put the notes into the Confidential Notebooks only, rather than into our own notebooks. Also, we were not allowed to tear any page from this notebook. In case we made mistakes when taking notes, we just crossed out the incorrect notes and kept the page

---

[63] I learned a couple of years later that every high school student's dossier would have a conclusion for the family background check. There were several different conclusions. For those, who got the conclusion "cannot be admitted," their dossiers would not be presented to the officers from the colleges' admission offices.

in the notebook. If we lost it, we must report to our leaders immediately. After the practice, we must submit our Confidential Notebooks to the college's confidential archive department. Later, we could borrow our own Confidential Notebooks if we need them in our future work, and return it after each use. It was said that this confidential management system was learned from the Soviet Union.

However, after this practice, I had never needed my Confidential Notebook in my future work because the information was out-dated when I started working.

The gate of the production area was guarded by the PLA soldiers. To enter the gate, we must wear our photo badges, which were issued by this corporation. We visited the blast furnace plant first, then the steel making plant, and finally the steel rolling plants. In addition, we also visited some auxiliary plants. We all enthusiastically observed the related equipment and became familiar with the production process, the equipment, and the environment.

In 1964 Beijing organized the performance "The East Red Music and Dancing Epic," performed by 3000 people, to celebrate the 15th anniversary of the founding of the PRC. The epic described the history of the Chinese Communist Party up to the time when the PRC was founded.[64] It was reported that this performance was proposed by Premier *Zhou Enlai,* who had previewed the performance many times and gave his feedback for revisions. The top composers, musicians, singers, choreographers, and dancers were called upon to participate, and people from the universities and factories in Beijing were also selected to perform. Mr. *Hu Jintao,* who became the President of the PRC years later, was the leader of the performance team of Tsinghua University.

When we were there in W-city, "The East Red Music and Dancing Epic" was performed by 1500 people, including the local professional musicians, singers, dancers, and other amateurs from the local universities and factories. We managed to buy the tickets and watched the show. The epic started with a group dancing accompanied by the music "The East

---

[64]   In her book "Mao the Unknown Story," Jung Zhang indicates that some events in the Long March, described in this epic and related history books, were not true.

is Red." The girls wearing sapphire blue skirts, with a yellow fan in each hand, danced around. When the music played the last lyric "Our Great Savior, he is" the girls made a sunflower-like tableau to express that Chinese people's love for Chairman Mao was like sunflowers towards the sun. At the end, the director turned to the audience and direct the audience to sing "The Internationale," together with the actors and actresses on the stage.

After completing our practice, we returned to G-city. Upon returning, I received a long letter from my younger brother. He said that after a few days of suffering and frustration, he started considering what to do next. One option was to join the Production and Construction Corps of *Ningxia*. He went to their recruiting office in Beijing and filled the application form. He waited until 9 p.m. when the officers returned from a meeting. After reviewing his application form, one of the officers told him with a smile: "We would warmly welcome you. Nevertheless, Beijing may be reluctant to let you guys leave. You can go home and wait for some further notification."

Sure enough, when he returned home, a notification from the Education Department of Beijing had been delivered. He was to be interviewed in an elementary school. During the interview, the interviewer listened to his self-introduction carefully. After that, the interviewer asked him whether he was interested in teaching in a middle school. My brother replied that he had been rejected by colleges, and might not be qualified. Nevertheless, the interviewer amiably advised him to be prepared for this new assignment.

A week later, he received another notification to attend a meeting in a Beijing Opera House. Getting there, he saw the interviewer had already been at the front door, and warmly welcomed him. During the meeting, an officer from the Education Department of Beijing announced that all students in this opera house, who were rejected by colleges due to the family background issues —more than 2000 in total —were hired by this department. There was a shortage of elementary and middle school teachers, and these rejected students were excellent academically, they were selected to become teachers.

The next day, there was a meeting for the schools to come and receive their assigned students. Most of the students were assigned jobs in elementary schools. When those students left with their corresponding employers, about 50 students stayed. These were the top students, and were assigned to teach in middle schools. My brother was one of them. They would be sent to some middle schools for training, and my brother was assigned to the Attached Middle School of Beijing University. Each student would have a mentor, and they would work together to prepare the classes and practice teaching.

I was elated by this good news and immediately sent a letter to Mama, with my brother's letter attached. In the reply to my brother, I gave him a quotation: "If you are an awl, even being put into a sack, you would be able to piercing it through to shine out." Years later, his diligent work rewarded him. He becomes the medal-winning Special-Grade Teacher[65] and invited by the Department of Education at the Vermont State University in 2000 to give lectures about teaching mathematics.

Near the end of 1965, the recorded Beijing performance of "The East is Red Epic" started showing in theaters nationwide. The songs in the epic immediately became a popular hit. Frequently I could hear people singing those songs on the campus.

In every New Year's Eve, our college would have a gala. The officers, faculty members, and students would perform. At the 1966 gala, the most performed songs were from "The East is Red Epic."

After the Chinese New Year in 1966, we went to W-city Heavy Machinery Factory for manufacturing practice. This factory was also built during the first five-year plan, with the help from the Soviet Union. Many engineers and workers had gone to the Soviet Union for training during the construction stage.

In the practice, we assisted the operators of various machine tools, to become familiar with the machining process of each specific machine tool.

After our production practice in W-city, we went to Shanghai for graduation practice. We were to visit the First, the Third, and the Fifth Steel Companies of Shanghai. After this practice, we would enter the last school year, and do our graduation design project. Then we would graduate and become engineers. We were all in high spirit.

After three days of travelling, we arrived at Shanghai. We were

---

[65]   This is the highest rank among the high school teachers.

arranged to live in the dormitory of Shanghai Steel School, a vocational school training various technician for the local steel industry. After implementing the "Adjust, Consolidate, Enhance, and Improve" policy from 63-65, China's economy recovered from the consequences of the Big Leap Forward, and started the third Five-Year plan in 1966. We noticed a lot of propaganda posters, as the third Five-Year plan seemed to be starting in high note in Shanghai.

At first, as planned, we were practicing with the workers in the repair and maintenance department. In addition to the daily work in the First Steel, we also spent a week working on the overhaul of a steel mill in the Fifth Steel.

One day in the late May, Professor *Chi*, who was in charge of our graduation practice, notified us to go to the Shanghai Steel School's conference room at 7 p.m. to hear some wonderful news. After diner, we all arrived the conference room early, and were eager to hear the good news. During the meeting, Professor *Chi* told us that the Beijing Design Institute of Iron & Steel had been assigned a project by the Ministry of Metallurgy to design an experimental steel factory using the most advanced steel making technologies at that time: the oxygen top-blown converter, or BOF for short, with continuous casting.[66] Due to the tight schedule, they needed additional hands.

We were easily noticed because, like all college students in China, we wore our college insignia. The student's insignia has red characters on a white background. The faculty member's insignia was white on a red background. After talking to us, the engineers from the institute learned that we were specialized in metallurgical machinery, and we're doing our graduation practice. So, they contacted Prof. *Chi* to discuss some possible cooperation. Prof. *Chi* reported this to the college leaders who thought this was an excellent opportunity for us to apply our knowledge in the real world. Moreover, such a project would also give us the opportunity of apprenticeship to learn from these experienced engineers. This news indeed made us overjoyed, and we all clapped thunderously.

The First Steel had an experimental BOF, and the Third Steel had an experimental equipment for continuous casting. Both were guarded by the

---

[66] Both of the techniques were commercialized during the early 1950s in the West.

PLA soldiers and required special permission to enter, because developing such advanced technology was confidential.

After a week or so, we received special permission, which was a green-colored photo badge. With this new badge, we went to the confidential BOF experiment area. The soldier carefully checked our badges one by one and let us enter. We were full of pride entering such a secure area because not many people had this privilege.

For the first few days, we listened to the lectures given by the senior engineers of The First Steel regarding the principle and the process of BOF. Then we started reading the blueprints of the equipment and observing the operations. At the end, we had a project to design an oxygen blowing mechanism. Because of the time limit, we were required to design and plot the assembly drawing only, without designing the components.

During that time, the Great Proletarian Cultural Revolution, or the Cultural Revolution for short, had been launched, and the atmosphere of political campaign intensified almost daily. At that time, a surprising debate occurred between the People's Daily and the PLA Daily. It was the first time in our lives to see two government newspapers openly expressing different opinions on a major issue. At that time, there was a slogan: "*Tu Chu Zheng Zhi* (emphasize politics, or ideology)." The People's daily published the editorial "Emphasizing politics should be incarnated into our daily work." But the PLA daily insisted that "emphasizing politics should be incarnated into thought revolution." After two editorials, People's Daily stopped further debating. But the PLA daily continued with their arguments, until the seventh editorial was published. The PLA Daily, as its name suggested, was mainly to serve the army, whereas the People's Daily was the mouthpiece of the Party and the central government. Because the People's Daily stopped debating after the second editorial, it seemed that the PLA daily won this debate. However, to many of us, "thought revolution" was still intangible and not incarnated into something concrete. We were all bewildered, not only by the outcome, but also by this unprecedented open debate by two official newspapers.

Another important article published at that time was "Comment on *San Jia cun* (Three Villages) – about counter-revolutionary features of *Yan Shan Ye Hua* (Nightly talks in *Yan* Mountain) and Notes of Three Villages" which denounced three scholars and writers in Beijing. Mr. *Yao*

Wenyuan,[67] the author of this commentary, was a rising political star at that time.

Busy with my engineering studies, I did not have time to read the works by so-called "Three Villages." But now the mandatory political study afforded me the time to read some of them, which were distributed as "reference materials for criticizing purposes." One of the most amazing articles was "*Yi Ge Ji Dan Di Jia Dang* (The Prospect of One Egg)." According to the original article, this was an ancient fable:

> A poor man picked up an egg on the road, he was elated
> and went back telling his wife: "We have property now!"
> "How?" The wife asked. He showed the egg and said:
> "I would ask somebody help me to hatch it. Then we
> would have a chicken. The chicken would lay more eggs,
> which in turn would produce more chickens. Several years
> later, we would be rich!"
> The wife was glad about the wonderful prospect.
> Then the guy was so carried away that he continued:
> "When I get rich, I can have many beautiful concubines!"
> Upon hearing this, his wife flared up and slapped the
> dreaming man on the face.
> "Ping!" The egg dropped to the ground. The egg was
> broken, together with his dream.

I could not figure out anything counter-revolutionary about the ancient fable. Yet, we were supposed to criticize it. So, we had to read the published articles that denounced this fable. As it turned out, this fable was accused as a disguised criticism against the Big Leap Forward. In 1958, the government announced that in 15 years or less, China would catch up with the U.K. Since the Big Leap Forward was followed by three years of famine, the author's toque-in-check, according to the critics, was that the government's goal of catching up with the U.K. in 15 years was like the egg dream of the poor man. It was not clear to me whether the author

---

[67] Mr. *Yao wenyuan* became one of the Gang of Four during the late stage of the Cultural Revolution, and was sentenced to 20 years in prison after the end of the Cultural Revolution.

had such intrigue in mind when he wrote this article, which is essentially a modern translation of the fable written in classical Chinese language. Nevertheless, this alleged goal was surely accomplished with the help of those critical remarks.

In addition, we were organized to watch some counter-revolutionary movies, one of them was "Sorrows of the Forbidden City", and the other was "Forced Recruitment." But just like the articles written by the "Three Villages," we were unable to see any serious political problem in these movies. Again, during the political study sessions, which was held one hour per day, we had to rely on reading the criticizing articles published in the newspapers to see the alleged political problems.

We were also organized to visit the exhibition of "Class Struggle Education" which showed visitors about the cruelty of capitalists. Shanghai was the most industrialized and commercialized city in China before the Liberation. There were a lot of private companies in Shanghai. In that exhibition, there were many photos and items on display, as the evidence of the exploitation. Two plates caught my attention. Both had a white background with dark purple characters, just like the street name plates in Shanghai those days. On one plate, the characters were "Share One Worker's Food by Two"; on the other were "Do Two Worker's Job by One." The narrator explained that the two plates were the evidence that the capitalist was cruel and exploitive because they wanted their workers to eat half and produce double.

One important event occurred during that time. The mayor of Beijing and three other high-ranking officers of the central government were denounced as an Anti-communist party clique, and removed from their posts. Also, the re-organized People's Daily published an editorial saying the Cultural Revolution was the revolution that would "touch people's souls." Only years later, did we realize what that means to ordinary people.

After finishing the BOF project, we went to Third Steel of Shanghai to learn about continuous casting. We went through a similar procedure as we did in the First Steel. It was late June when we were enthusiastically working on the design project.

Before we finished the draft, Prof. *Chi* held a meeting in a conference room, and read a telegram from our college leadership. The telegram asked us to stop the practice and return immediately, to take part in the Cultural Revolution. Upon hearing the news, everybody was disappointed and nobody said anything. I felt like attending a splendid banquet, but was ordered to leave after just tasting a couple of delicious appetizers.

When we were back to our school, Mr. *Han*, the party secretary of the college, had a meeting with us. He said that the Cultural Revolution was an important political campaign, and that we must attend. Hopefully when the campaign ended in a couple of months, as was typical of all previous political campaigns, we could go back to Shanghai and continue with our graduation projects. Although we all felt that this new political campaign was unusual, no one in the room could imagine that the Cultural Revolution would run out of control. So, a telegram was sent to the Beijing Design Institute of Iron & Steel saying that in late October or early November, we would finish the political campaign, and could continue with the design project.

Returning to the school, we walked around the campus, and noticed that some new temporary booths were set up on both sides of the roads for posting so-called "Big Character Posters", which were written with the traditional writing brush and with character size of 2-3 inches.

The targets of the Big Character Poster were professors, especially senior professors, because at the early stage of the Cultural Revolution, the main targets were "bourgeois reactionary academic authorities." The professors, who were educated before the Liberation, and included some who also had studied in the West, were regarded as bourgeois intellectuals. Since the senior professors were more or less academically authoritative, they seemed to fit better to the category of bourgeois reactionary "academic authorities." In addition, those who had historical problems, such as those who had worked for the Kuomintang's government, or had joined Kuomintang or its youth organizations, or were labeled as the "rightist" in 1957, etc. were also condemned on the big character posters.

The first shocking news we heard, after returning to the campus, was that Professor *Chen* had hanged himself, because he was among those targeted in the Big Character Posters.

During Mao's era, committing suicide was regarded as

counterrevolutionary. The logic went like this: people were the happiest in the world under the communist leadership and the happy people would never kill themselves. If one committed suicide, then he or she practically expressed some dissatisfaction, or even anger, towards the leadership of the Party, therefore was a counter-revolutionist.

Professor *Chen* was labeled as a "rightist", or was "put on a rightist cap," as it was normally called. Since his problem was not as serious as others, he was able to keep teaching, with reduced salary. After that his wife divorced him and brought their children to Hong Kong.

Professor *Chen* taught the Theoretical Mechanics class. His lectures were welcomed by students because of the rigorous logic and clear presentation. His "rightist cap" was removed in 1960 due to his hard working and sincere self-criticism. Nevertheless, like many rightists, he was targeted again in this new political campaign because he became one of the "de-caped rightists," those who were rightists before and later rehabilitated. There were more such phrases these days: when an inmate served the sentence and was released, this person would receive a new title: *Lao Gai Shi Fang Fan* (formal criminal). These new titles sounded oxymoron, but it reflected the political reality at that time.

In Chinese, *Yun Dong* means sports, and also means a political campaign. Those who once fell into a political hole were jokingly called *Yun Dong Yuan*, which literally means an athlete, but figuratively refers to those unfortunate fellows, who once were in political trouble and would always be the first to bear the brunt when a new political campaign came –just like athletes whose profession would require them to participate every sport event. Finding himself had become a *Yun Dong Yuan*, Prof. *Chen* must have despaired, and totally lost his faith in life.

As usual, his suicide was regarded as counter-revolutionary, and the college leaders called an all-hands meeting to denounce Prof. *Chen*. During the meeting, a leader enumerated many of his anti-party "crimes." Among them was writing a counter-revolutionary poem. The leader started to read Prof. *Chen*'s alleged counter-revolutionary poem. The first two lines were:

"Ten years of separation by life and death,
How can I forget it even I am not thinking about it?"

"He was labeled as a Rightist in 1957, now is the tenth year since then, he still held great hatred toward the Party!" The leader asserted.

...

Upon hearing this, some of my classmates and I were stunned because this poem was written not by Prof. *Chen*, but by *Su Shi*, a famous poet (Jan. 8, 1037 to Aug. 24, 1101 A.D.) in *Song* dynasty. The poem was written to commemorate the ten- year anniversary of the death of his young wife, who died at the age of 27. We looked each other in disbelief, but nobody dared to say anything.

After the meeting, we continued to participate the Cultural Revolution by writing Big Character Posters. Our college was engineering-oriented, and all the professors had a technical background. It was extremely difficult to associate technical lessens with politics or ideology. We could not find much to write about. Yet, we were supposed to carry out the Cultural Revolution, and we must manage to criticize professors politically.

After some difficulties, we wrote one poster as follows: the physical laws were discovered by the proletarian class, therefore the physical laws, such as Newton's Laws, should not be named after a specific scientist. Calling those laws by the Western scholars' names, reflected their admiration to capitalist scholars. Therefore, their ideology was bourgeois and should be criticized.

When we were in the great boredom in making up those Big-Character Posters to fulfill our so-called "political tasks" assigned by the college leaders, the news came to our rescue: Chairman Mao swam across the Yangtze River, and he called on the young people "to swim in the river and the ocean when the wind is strong and the wave is high". This phrase had both literary and figurative meanings. Literally, it meant, as suggested by the words, to swim not in the swimming pool, but in real wild water, when the wind was strong and the wave was high. Its figurative meaning was to actively participate in the nationwide political campaign, currently the Cultural Revolution. But we all emphasized the literal meaning of Chairman Mao's words, and went to swim daily in the afternoon. After the noon nap, we would go to the nearby river to swim until the diner time. The city government also organized a citywide activity: learn from

Chairman Mao to swim across a river. Most of us happily participated and enjoyed it.

Entering August of 1966, the situation became more dramatic. On August 10, the radio reported a news, saying Chairman Mao visited a government's Mass Reception Station in Beijing, and told the people there:

"You should pay close attention to the national events, and carry through the Cultural Resolution!"

This was quite unusual because it was the first time Chairman Mao ever did this after the Liberation.

Two days later, the party issued a document about the Cultural Revolution. Since it contained 16 articles, it was commonly called "Sixteen Articles" for short. A new organization, the Central Cultural Revolution Group (CCRG), was set up to lead this new political campaign. Mr. *Chen Boda* was appointed as the head, Mao's wife *Jiang Qing* as the deputy, and Mr. *Kang Sheng* was the consultant.

The college leaders immediately organized us to study this document. In this document, the term "Capitalist Roader" was used again after its first appearance in the "23 Articles" for *the Si Qing* campaign. However, the document still did not give the accurate definition of this term. The document just stated that the main goal of the Cultural Revolution was to strike the "Capitalist Roader." After studying the document, I thought that only officers had the power to decide which road to take. We ordinary citizens had no power. So, perhaps the main target of this political campaign was not the ordinary people. This made me feel slight relief, but I was still not certain.

Sure enough, the slight relief was short lived. At that time, newspaper reported that a Red Guard movement was developing in Beijing. It was initiated in some middle schools. The member of those organizations would wear a red armband with "Red Guard" printed on it.

On August 18, there was a huge gathering in Tiananmen Square. Chairman Mao, wearing military uniform, reviewed Red Guards of Beijing. After the Liberation, Chairman Mao had always worn a gray Mao suit in public events. So, this was the first time we saw Mao wearing the PLA uniform. This might send out some unusual signal.

During the rally, one female representative of the Red Guard of Beijing put a Red Guard armband on Mao's left sleeve. It was reported that

Chairman Mao asked her name, she answered that her name was *Song Binbin*.

"Which *Binbin*, *binbin* the elegance?"

"Yes."

"That is not good, *yaowu ma* (be violent)."

There was a rumor that she later changed her name to *Song Yaowu*[68], as suggested by Chairman Mao.

This news made the Red Guard movement quickly spread to the whole nation. It was in this mass gathering, Mr. *Lin Biao* showed up as the vice chairman of the CPC, replacing Mr. *Liu Shaoqi* to become Mao's new lieutenant. Newspapers started calling *Lin Biao* as Chairman Mao's "closest comrade-in-arms." After August 18, 1966 Chairman Mao conducted seven more reviews of the Red Guards coming from all parts of China.

After the 8-18 event, the Central Radio Station started to repeatedly broadcast Chairman Mao's old work, written in 1927: "The Report on Hunan Peasant Movement." This paragraph was most quoted at that time:

> "A revolution is not like inviting people to dinner, writing
> an article, painting a picture, or doing embroidery. It
> cannot be so gentle, nice, courteous, tolerant, and yielding.
> A revolution is an insurrection, and is the violent action
> for one class to overthrow another class."

As a result, rudeness and violence were in fashion. The ruder and the more violent one behaved, the more revolutionary one would demonstrate. A slogan appeared in Beijing: "Long live the Red Terror!"

This slogan signaled a milestone in the Cultural Revolution. It was during the time of the Red Terror that my maternal grandmother was driven out of Beijing. By the time of the Liberation, my maternal grandparents had inherited the amount of land that met the criterion for the Landlord Class. As with other landlords, the properties of their family were confiscated and re-distributed. However, even no longer having any

---

[68] *Song Binbin* later studied in and immigrated to the United States. She denied that she changed her name.

property, she still had been wearing the "Landlord" cap. To clean up the capital city politically, the people of the black types were to be driven out of Beijing. So, my grandmother was ordered to leave. At that time, she was more than 80 years old, with binding feet, it was difficult for her to travel alone. With permission, my cousin, the oldest daughter of my younger uncle, was allowed to escort her back to her hometown in J-province. When the train stopped at one station for transfer, some Red Guards boarded the train to check the passengers. They notice that Grandma was from Beijing and guessed that she must have been one of the black types, being kicked out of Beijing. They immediately ordered my grandma to get out. On the platform, a denouncing meeting started. After shouting some revolutionary slogans, they used the scissors to cut her hair into the so-called "*Ying Yang* Head:" one half of her hair was cut, and the other half remained. They also brushed black ink on her whole face so that she would be surely recognized as one of the black types. Then they allowed her to board a train leaving for her home town. After helping Grandma to board the train, my cousin was ordered to board another train back to Beijing, and was no longer allowed to accompany Grandma.

In 1968, Grandma came to N-city and lived with us for a couple of months. She told me her ordeal in details. She continued her trip after my cousin left. When reached the destination, Grandma was notified to get out by the railroad staff. Standing on the platform, she did not know what to do, what she did was to keep praying. Fortunately, an acquaintance happened to pass by. He recognized Grandma and led her to my fourth aunt's (her fourth daughter's) home.

"So, Jesus came to my rescue." She smiled: "I might have died without the help from the Lord."

Around that time, a Beijing college student, called *Tan Lifu*, gave a speech which became well-circulated. The key idea was best expressed in an antithetical couplet group. In Chinese, such an antithetical couplet group is mainly used as a form of calligraphic arts. It consists of two vertical scrolls which form an antithesis. There is one horizontal scroll, in most cases consisting four characters, which somewhat sums up the words in the two vertical scrolls. The couplet group is also used as a poetic literature form to tersely express some theme.

In *Tan*'s antithetical couplet group, the first scroll said the son of a revolutionary hero was also a revolutionary star. The second said the son of a counter-revolutionary was a bastard. The horizontal scroll was: Basically So.

As mentioned earlier, the family background was determined in the early 1950s. Now the family background was further categorized into two types. The family background of the Landlord, the Rich peasant, the Capitalist and those families with family members or relatives being the counter-revolutionist, the bad element, and the rightist, were called "Black Types." There were three types of family background that I had not heard before: the families of revolutionary officers, who had worked in the communist government before the Liberation; the revolutionary soldier, who was a Red Army or the PLA solider before the Liberation; the revolutionary martyr, who died for the communist party. Together with the families of the Working Class, the Poor and Lower-Middle Peasant Class, these family backgrounds were of "Red Types."

With Tan's speech spreading, the younger generation of the Black families was called *Gou Zai Zi*, which literally means a puppy, but in this context, it means the son or daughter of a bastard. It became a common practice to ask one's family background, even when one was shopping. In such situation, those who were from the Red families would answer the question loudly and proudly. But those who were from the black families would answer the question with lowered heads and voices, and also would be treated rudely.

Naturally, only those who were from red families were qualified to become Red Guards.

It was said that some influential high ranking officers gave speeches in 1961-1962 and emphasized that student grades were as important as military skills of the soldier. A soldier who was Red, but had bad military skills could not be regarded as a good soldier. Likewise, students, who was bad in their study, could not be regarded as good students. Therefore, a student's performance on the entrance examination should be treated as important as the political background in the college admission. As a result, many students from black families were admitted in 1962.

When the Red Guard group was organized in our class, only five students were marginally qualified. Some of them were from red families, but with problematic social relations, some were from "neutral" families, i.e. they were not from the families of red types, nor were they from the families of black types, such as the middle peasant (not the Lower-Middle peasant class). Due to my father's issue, I was disqualified to wear the Red Guard armband. This made me and most of my classmates depressed. Without the Red Guard armband, we would feel like second class citizens, when walking on the street.

One of the "Sixteen Article states: "The Cultural Revolution group, the Cultural Revolution committee, the Cultural Revolution congress are the best organizations under the communist party's leadership (for people) to educate themselves... The members of those organizations should be elected like the way did in the Paris Commune. Candidates should be proposed and discussed by the mass and then the candidates should be voted." As a result, our class also prepared to set up the Cultural Revolution group. During that time, people started to examine the possible candidates. It was natural that the family background was given the top priority in this process. Some classmates, who had better family backgrounds, were listed as the candidates. Mr. *Hu* had a family background of the Poor Peasant Class, so he was elected as the head of our Cultural Revolution group.

Gradually an activity called "*DA chuanlian* (big linkups)" started. The Red Guards could travel around the country, free of charge, to spread the "Cultural Revolution Fire." The first Red Guard came to our college was from Beijing University. In late May1966, Ms. *Nie Yuanzi*, the party secretary of the Department of Philosophy at Beijing University, and another six faculty members, wrote a Big Character Poster attacking the leaders of this university. Chairman Mao called it "the first Marxist-Leninist Big Character Poster" and was broadcasted to the whole nation. In the meantime, Chairman Mao also wrote the new inscription for Beijing University: "*Xin Bei Da* (New Beijing University)". This inscription was published on the front page of all newspapers. Because of this, when this red guard of Beijing University came to our college, he was treated as if he were an imperial envoy. He was invited to give a speech in our auditorium. During the speech, he declared: "Our Great Leader wrote a new inscription for our university and I have brought it here!" Then he pulled out a roll of paper, open it, lift it high, as if holding a piece of holy paper. A Thunderous applause broke out while he was walking on the stage from one side to the other.

I thought perhaps he really had the original, so I ran close to the stage to take a good look at it. I found it was just the piece of newspaper with the published Mao's inscription on it.

After that, more Red Guard units came, frequently in groups, and many of them were young students from high schools and middle schools. At first, they were also invited to give speeches. But later we found their speeches were more or less similar, and were echoes of the newspapers. So, there were no more such speeches in the auditorium.

Those Red Guards also brought some mimeographed "leaders' speeches," which were manually recorded speeches given by the members of the Central Cultural Resolution Group in the Beijing's high schools and universities. Those speeches were not officially published. So, the "leaders' speeches" brought us a lot more information than the newspapers and magazines. As a result, those mimeographed leaders' speeches were quickly mimeographed again and distributed as circulars in the city streets. It was quite common during that time that when someone held up a stack of such circulars, people would scramble to grab them, because everyone was eager to acquire more information about this "unprecedented and soul-touching" political campaign.

Inspired by those Red Guards from Beijing, some students became excited. In the open space in front of the student dining hall, they stood on a podium, made from dining tables, and gave speeches like in movies of May Forth Movement in 1919. By that time, the CPC had published nine commentaries criticizing the Soviet Communist Party (SCP) and had denounced SCP as the Revisionist. All college students were organized to study these commentaries, known as "Nine Commentaries". As a result, the highlights of those student speeches were echoing Nine Commentaries.

> "Now our country has entered a critical anti-revisionist moment, we must save our country!"
> "We must purify our country with Marxism-Leninism and Mao Zedong thought!"
> "We cannot let our country go down the revisionist road!"
> "We cannot let our country change color!"

"We must keep our motherland in the red color forever!"

...

It was said that John Dulles, the former secretary of the state, in a speech predicted that the Communist Camp, the countries governed by communist parties and headed by the Soviet Union, would change color, i.e. change its ideology from communist to capitalist, in the third or fourth generation. Chairman Mao said that we would let this prediction go bust. This was why the students who spoke centered on this topic.

Also, some "Mao Zedong Thought Propaganda Teams," a kind of a performing arts group, came to our campus. The most popular form of the performance was the rhymed dialogue between two performers, one male and one female. The male student first spoke a sentence and then made a corresponding stage gesture. Then the girl spoke another sentence and showed a different stage gesture, together they formed a statue-like tableau. The content was revolutionary and the gestures were masculine. Both performers wore old military uniforms without military insignia. The uniforms were from family members or relatives, who were serving or once had served in the PLA. The older the better because older uniform showed seniority of their family members or relatives. This was the most respected and admired attire at that time.

One day, a Mao Zedong Thought propaganda team performed a part of the revolutionary ballet "The Red Detachment of Women." In one scene, there was a sign "The proletariat can only liberate themselves after they have liberated all mankind." This well-known proposition was shortened from a section in the preface of the 1888 edition of The Communist Manifesto. After the performance, we went back to our dormitory. On the way back, I overheard some discussions near me.

> "Would all mankind include class enemies, such as landlords, rich peasants, counter-revolutionists, bad elements, capitalists, and rightists?" One asked.
> "Of course, by biological definition, they are all human beings." Another student answered.
> "Then, based on the Marx's words, we should also liberate the class enemies?"

The conversation went into silence. Nobody would stick their neck out to answer such a thorny question.

"In my opinion," another one broke out the silence," landlords, rich peasants, counter-resolutions, bad elements, capitalists, and rightists are not included in mankind."

"Why?"

"Because they are *Niu Gui She Shen*!"

"Niu Gui She Shen" is a Chinese phrase literally means "cow demons and snake spirits." But these words became the nickname for all class enemies after Chairman Mao used the phrase in such a sense. By using the figurative meaning of the phrase in this way, this college student excluded those class enemies from mankind, therefore they would not qualify for liberation. Although this argument had the logic problem of disguised replacement of the concept, but nobody dared to rebuke this holier than pope attitude. Indeed, based on this logic, it was quite common to treat those "cow ghosts and snake spirits" inhumanly in those days.

Among the leaders' speeches, the most important was perhaps the "Bombard the headquarters –My Big Character Poster," said to be written by Chairman Mao on August 5. The implied target of this poster was the president Liu, without actually naming him. In this context, the word "bombard" did not mean using real bombs or cannons. It meant figuratively to attack or denounce someone, and was most frequently used in the second half of 1966.

Mentioning this Big Character Poster, the red guards from other places criticized that the political campaign in our city was "too soft, too gentle, and lack of revolutionary atmosphere." They told us that if Chairman Mao bombarded the highest headquarter, then we should follow Chairman Mao's lead to bombard local headquarters.

One day in early September, all students at the three universities in the city, and students from some middle schools marched to the county district office building, pulling the party secretary of the county out of his office, and standing on a table. He was asked to acknowledge that he did not actively lead the Cultural Revolution, and should do a self-criticism in front of Chairman Mao's portrait. He did this and also promised that he would follow Chairman Mao's teaching, and more actively lead this soul-touching campaign. Then students walked away.

At that time, my elder uncle, who taught at H-province Teacher's Institute, sent me a letter. With 1957 anti-rightist campaign still fresh in his memory, he warned me never to show off bravery to bombard party leaders. He saw with his own eye that some young people responded to the call to criticize the Party in 1957 and became rightists, then they all suffered miserably. My heart sank, after reading the letter. I could not fall asleep that night. I was torn between the two opposite options: to rebel, as we did a few days ago when we bombarded the county headquarter, I would have the risk to become a rightist or even a counter-revolutionist; but not to rebel, I would take the risk of not following Chairman Mao's call for bombarding capitalist roaders. This could also have grave political consequences. It was not clear which was more dangerous.

To choose a safer option, I carefully and repeatedly studied each joint editorial by the People's Daily, the PLA's Daily and the Red Flag magazine, referred to as "two newspapers and one magazine," to grasp anything that was not only directly said, but also implied between the lines. In addition, we also read as many "Leaders' speeches" as we could get, in the hope that those speeches could give us some additional clues about the Cultural Revolution. Actually, everybody tried desperately to obtain information, or even rumors.

During Chairman Mao's second review of the Red Guard on August 31, Premier *Zhou Enlai* announced that the government would pay for all college students to come to Beijing, to learn how the Cultural Revolution was carried out in the capital city. In Mao's era, traveling was very expensive, compared with people's income. Most people never got a chance to visit the capital cities of their provinces, let alone the capital city of China. Naturally, we were all overjoyed upon hearing this news.

Near the end of September, our college received the notification that it was our turn to go to Beijing. After three days of travel, we arrived at the Beijing railroad station. Then buses took us to the University of Science and Technology of China in the west of Beijing[69].

My younger brother was still in the Attached Middle School of Beijing University for training. I used the public phone to call my brother's school,

---

[69]   This university moved to Hefei in Anhui province in 1970.

telling him that I was in Beijing. We decided to meet at the front gate of the University of Science and Technology. My brother told me that biking might take 30-40 minutes.

We had not seen each other since 1960, and when we met, I could barely recognize him. In the past six years, he had become a full-blown young man, from a sheepish boy. We looked at each other and shook hands joyfully. Then, we went out for a long walk, and exchanged the latest information about the Cultural Revolution. The first thing we discussed was the warning given by our elder uncle. My brother could not figure out a good solution either. Based on the information we had so far, we still could not decide whether this political campaign was the same as the 1957 anti-rightist campaign or not. So, we agreed that for the time being, the safest way for us was to state neutral and low-key. In the cases that we had to select a side, then stay with the majority.

My brother also told me the news about our younger uncle. To my astonishment, this very uncle, a representative of the National People's Congress of China, was locked up in a "cowshed." One of the charges was that he was an American spy. When the Red Guards searched his home during the "Wipe out Four Olds (old ideas, old culture, old customs, and old habits) and Establish Four News (new ideas, new culture, new customs, and new habits)" campaign, they found knives, forks and spoons with "U.S.N." engraved on the stick. That was regarded as the spy evidence. The fact was that when this uncle studied in Minnesota, he sometimes went to garage sales. Once he saw those nice stainless-steel knives, forks, and spoons, sold very cheaply in a garage sale, he happily bought all of them so that he could use some of them and give the rest to relatives as souvenirs, because utensils made of stainless steel were extremely rare in China.

My uncle could not explain all the details to young Red Guides who had never lived in the United States.

Facing such an overwhelming red terror, nobody dared to be on its way. It was said that someone who waved the book of the Chinese Constitution to protest a raid by the Red Guards, then the Constitution booklet was immediately taken by the Red Guards and torn into pieces. Actually, under red terror, the simple fact that my uncle studied in the United States, the number one imperialistic country, could be enough to charge him as an American spy. Likewise, some, who studied in the Soviet Union, which was regarded as the "Revisionist" country, were charged as the Soviet spies during that period.

However, I was still puzzled: how could there be "cowsheds" on the campus of an engineering college? As it turned out, it was not a real cowshed. Those "cowsheds" were just ordinary classrooms. Since the inmates were "cow ghosts and snake spirits," those classrooms were called "cowsheds" derogatorily. Locking up people not by any juristic organization, without any legal procedure, was called Dictatorship by the Masses. Such a Mass Dictatorship was common these days, and quickly spread to other parts of the country. Every unit had some "cowsheds" to lock up those who were regarded as class enemies.

On the second day when we arrived in Beijing, each of us was given a transportation pass that allowed us to take buses and trolleybuses in Beijing, free of charge. This was to facilitate us to visit different universities and institutions to learn how the Cultural Revolution was implemented in the capital city. I used this pass to visit many universities and research institutions to read the Big Character Posters there.

When I first visited Beijing in 1960, people waiting for buses were automatically formed a line and got on the buses in an orderly way. Now, no bus station had any line, only crowds. Once a bus came, people would swamp to the door, and the most physically fit would get on first. Because of the crowds, when squeezing into the bus, I lost my fountain pen, which was the gift from Mama for attending the college, and it cost more than a half of her monthly salary.

One day, I teamed up with Mr. *Liu*, a classmate to go to *Wangfujing* in the downtown of Beijing, where some cultural organizations were located. We took the bus to get there and then walked along the *Wangfujing* Street. We first saw the Cultural Association of China and decided to pay a visit. Entering the door, we saw a big billboard with red background and golden characters, which were the Chairman Mao's words:

"Using novels to undertake anti-Party activities is a big invention by *Hu Feng*."

Mr. *Hu Feng*[70] was a well-known writer who was labeled as a counter-revolutionist in 1955. There were many pictures and excerpts of *Hu Feng's* writings on display to show his alleged counter-revolutionary crimes.

After that, we continued walking along the street, southbound, and soon an exhibition caught our attention: "Exhibition of *Huang Zhou's* counter-revolutionary black paints." Mr. *Huang* was an eminent painter good at portraying donkeys. Wondering how donkey paintings could be used as tools to engage in counter-revolutionary activities, we decided to take a look.

When we reached the front door, two young girls wearing "Red Guard" armbands stopped us.

> "Are you Red Guards?" Apparently not. Neither of us wore "Red Guard" armband.
> "Are you from the families of the Red Types?"
> I looked at *Liu* and see what he would say, because he was quick-witted.
> "No." He lowered his head and answered honestly.
> "No." I followed suit.
> "Then you are not qualified to see the exhibition," one girl said coldly.
> Walking away reluctantly and bitterly, I asked *Liu* why he had not dared to say we were from the families of Red Types. "After all, the girls did not know us. How could they know we were not from the families of Red Types?"
> "In case they ask us to show our student IDs and write down our names for verification, we could be in great political trouble by pretending to be from Red families. Such a risk was not worth taking," Mr. *Liu* answered.

While staying in Beijing, I also visited Ba Bao Shan, the well-known revolutionary cemetery. When high ranking leaders pass away, their ashes would be buried here. I heard this cemetery many times on the radio and also read about it from the newspaper. Now I had the opportunity to see this famous cemetery with my own eyes.

---

70   Mr. *Hu Feng* was rehabilitated in 1988, after the end of the Cultural Revolution.

With the free transportation pass, I got there by bus. Upon entering it, I was surprised to see a big white marble tombstone broken into pieces on the ground. Those buried here were all veteran revolutionaries and martyrs. How could their tombstone be destroyed like this? I looked at the name on the tombstone: *Qu Qiubai*, once a general secretary of the CPC in the 1920s. This made me recall that about two months earlier in a leader's speech, he was denounced as a traitor because he wrote his last remark, *"Duo Yu De Hua* (redundant words)," before he was executed. This remark was among the mimeographed materials brought to us by the Beijing Red Guards.

In this remark, he stated:

> "With my personality, ability, knowledge, to be a leader in the Chinese Communist Party is a historical misunderstanding," and "I had already left the pioneer team of the proletarian class, stopped political struggle, put down my weapon, if you – the comrades in the communist party – could have heard all I wrote down here, you should have expelled me from the Party... You already have the right to regard me as a kind of traitor."

The words impressed me the most were the following description about himself:

> "A weak and thin horse pulling a heavy truck up a stiff hill a step by a step. It was impossible to retreat, but climbing further would beyond his ability. That was what I felt when I was a political leader."

I felt a strong compassion when reading this remark. At the end of his remark, he also expressed strong desire to read some well-known novels, such as "Dream of the Red Chamber." He was only 36 years old when he was executed. He had demonstrated great talent in literature and translation, and was a good friend of the famous writer *Lu Xun*. Because of these words and other comments in his remark, he was denounced as a traitor by some of the central leaders, and in1972 he was formally named as a traitor.[71]

---

[71] He was rehabilitated in 1979, after the Cultural Revolution.

The broken tombstone reminded me why Father wanted us to stay away from the political arena. Once involved, there seems no way out. Not only could one lose one's life, but such a person could also be insulted even in the tomb.

As part of Class Education, we visited the exhibition of "Court Yard of Collecting Rents" in the Palace Museum. This was a group of life-sized clay sculptures telling the exploiting and oppressing story of the cruel landlord Mr. *Liu Wencai* in *Sichuan* province. The sculptures were praised by the People's Daily as "the peak of the proletarian arts." One leader even called it "the atomic bomb in Chinese artistic circle." Together with the movie "White Hair Girl," and the novel "Rooster Crowed at midnight," the trio became well-known materials in class struggle education, to show "Crows are black everywhere in the world," meaning every member of the exploitive class in this world was cruel without exception.[72] This exhibition started in 1965 and fueled unprecedented hatred toward all class enemies, their family members, and offspring.

However, near the end of our stay in Beijing, we found some changes toward the matter of family background. We heard that Mr. *Chen Boda*, the head of the CCRG, criticized *the Tan's speech* as reactionary bloodline theory. *Jiang Qing*, also suggested a revision to *Tan*'s couplet:

The first scroll: A son of a revolutionary hero should take over (the revolutionary cause).

The second scroll: A son of a counter-revolutionist should rebel (their parents).

The horizontal scroll: should be so.

This modification started to have some influence upon the on-going Cultural Revolution. As a result, some mass organizations appeared in the university campuses in Beijing. Unlike Red Guard organizations, these new mass organizations no longer admitted the members based on their family backgrounds. Instead, as long as one agreed with the organization's main opinions regarding the Cultural Resolution, one could join, regardless of family background. During that period, the students broke into two major

---

[72] In 1990s and later, some researchers published articles saying the trio were faked or distorted from the truth.

factions. One faction was the rebel who made the communist leaders as the target. The other faction wanted to protect those leaders and to focus their target on the Black Types. This faction was initially called "defending emperor" faction by the rebel. But later, advised by the CCRG, this faction was called the conservative faction.

October 1, the National Day, was coming, and we were arranged to parade through Tiananmen Square and see Chairman Mao with our own eyes. This made everyone excited. In the evening on September 30, each of us received a lunch pack. Around 11:00 p.m., we all boarded buses and went across the city to the east part of Beijing. Then we got off the buses and marched to *Chang-An* Boulevard, the east-west main street passing through Tiananmen Square. At that time, rarely any college student had a watch, so we could only guess the time by observing the stars. When we walked to the assigned spot, Venus appeared, it was close to dawn.

Finally, the ceremony started. After speeches by vice Chairman *Lin Biao* and Premier *Zhou Enlai*, we started parading slowly.

Near noon, we arrived at Tiananmen Square. Upon entering it, everybody started waving the small red book of Mao's Quotation, and shouting at the top capacity of our lungs in unison: "Long Live Chairman Mao!"

From the street, it was no way to see the faces of the leaders standing on the Rostrum which was a couple of hundred yards away. I could only guess that the one, wearing a gray Mao suit and standing at the center, must be Chairman Mao. The one on his left side and wearing a green military uniform must be *Lin Biao*, and the one on Mao's right side and wearing a gray Mao suit, must be Premier *Zhou Enlai*.

After passing Tiananmen Square, we were led to the campus of the Central Conservatory of Music. After eating the food in our lunch packs, we took a nap. Without sleeping for the whole night, we were all exhausted and our voices became hoarse due to the fanatical shouting. So soon we fell asleep on the ground. Just around 6 p.m., we returned to Tiananmen Square again for the evening fireworks show. It was the first time in my life to see live fireworks show in such a close distance, and was a wonderful experience.

During our stay in Beijing, we also learned about the working group in the universities sent by Mr. *Liu Shaoqi* were disbanded. Students searched for "black materials" the working group had collected. They found each person has a specific dossier which mainly recorded their words that were regarded as politically incorrect or even counter-revolutionary. The students were angry after reading those files, and burned them.

A couple of days after the National Day celebration, we returned to our college. Due to the new trend in Beijing, our college also followed suit to set up a mass organization: *Dong Fang Hong Zhan Dou Tuan* (the East Red Regiment). Commander Mr. *Sun* was a student in the Department of Mining and Mineral Processing, and had entered the college also in 1962. The Deputy Commander *Tang* was from our Department, and he had entered the college in 1965. The vast majority of the students, professors, and office workers were members of this Regiment. The main thrust of this organization was to follow Chairman Mao's direction: to rebel against the capitalist roader. There was also a conservative group: Mao Zedong Thought Combat Team, which consisted about less than five percent of the total people in the college.

Now I was in the critical moment of choosing wisely, but there was no safe option. I was once more torn between the two dangerous choices. It was out of the question to be a 'fence sitter' because this would get me attacked by both factions. Recalling that when in Beijing, in addition to seeing the Chairman Mao's Poster: "Bombard the Headquarter," I also learned another new Supreme instruction:

"Rebel is justified."

Even some music had been added to make this instruction a quotation song. Perhaps this time it was really different from the 1957 anti-rightist campaign. And since the vast majority of the people in the college had joined the East Red Regiment, it seemed safer to stay with the larger group, as discussed with my brother in Beijing. So, I joined the East Red Regiment, together with the vast majority of my classmates. Each class was a "combat team" in this regiment. Since the majority of the people in the college were in East Red Regiment, the leaders of the college were sidelined after they were bombarded, and the student leaders in the regiment actively led the Cultural Revolution.

In the early November, we received a telegram from the Beijing Design Institute of Iron & Steel, asking us to return to Shanghai and to continue with the design project. The head of our class, now called "combat team," held a meeting and announced this news. It had been decided by those leaders that we would go to Shanghai in a few days.

However, at that moment a classmate stood up, and said that the Cultural Revolution had not ended and was now in a critical moment. How could we not to continue with this soul-touch revolution, as advocated by Chairman Mao, and to go for the design work? I looked at Mr. *Zhan*, the top leader of our "combat team," and hoped that he still decided to go. But he lowered his head, pondered for a while and finally decided to call off this trip. I realized that in such case, not to carry out the Cultural Revolution could be an extremely serious ideological mistake, which nobody dared to make. Mr. *Zhan* told another member of the group leaders to send a telegram to the Beijing Design Institute of Iron & Steel, telling them that we must continue with the Cultural Revolution and could not work with them anymore.

I was really upset yet helpless. This classmate was not a member of the communist youth league, nor was he from the Red Type families. I was puzzled why he would be so enthusiastic about this damn political campaign. After the meeting, I talked to this classmate. He told me that it was true that he was from a black family, but this revolution provided an opportunity to thoroughly change the fate. He said:

> "If I die for this revolution, I would be a martyr, my family could be upgraded to a Red Type. If I survived to the victory, I would be a part of revolutionary officer, so my children's family background would also be of a Red Type."

But I was not so sure about the outcome of this revolution, and thought he had screwed up this excellent learning opportunity.

Entering 1967, the situation became more turbulent. In January, Shanghai rebelling organizations seized the power of Shanghai party and government. They announced the establishment of Shanghai Commune, whose name would be changed to the Shanghai Revolutionary Committee later. This event was the headline news of all newspapers and was hailed as "January Storm". From then on, the Seizure of Power was at the center stage of the Cultural Revolution. When a new provincial Revolution

Committee was established, a salute telegram was sent to Chairman Mao. Then the telegram was published as headline news, and broadcasted from central and local radio stations.

However, the process in other provinces was not as smooth as that in Shanghai. Fighting between different mass organizations broke out due to different opinions and other issues. Each faction accused the other organizations as the ones against Chairman Mao's revolutionary line. Each organization would find some Mao's quotations which supported their opinions. Since there was no way for any organization to win the debate, gradually physical force was used to fight one another. In late May, one student of our college was beaten to death when he and a group of other students tried to take over the wired broadcast station of G-city. He was the first casualty in this city since the Cultural Revolution started. Next day, there was a mass demonstration in the city. All the organizations sharing the same opinions as the East Red Regiment had some people attended this demonstration, by carrying the body of this dead student. The situation became increasingly grave and the political campaign in this city showed the initial sign of out of control.

Learning that somebody in our college died in a fight, my sister was anxious and came to see me. Due to the situation, I suggested that she go back to N-city as soon as possible. But it was too late. Along the way to the long distance bus station, there were several factories which were the opponents of our college. They would detain and beat anyone looking like a student. She had to stay.

During that period, we heard that comrade *Jiang Qing*, the deputy of CCRG, had proposed a new slogan "*Wen Gong Wu Wei* (Attack with the pen and defend with the weapon)." In one of the mimeographed leaders' speeches, it was said that Chairman Mao had prepared, like he did in 1927, to go back to *Jinggang* Mountain to start another guerrilla war against Capitalist Roaders. "Following Chairman's footsteps for a guerrilla war" became a popular slogan.

Our opponents were supported by the G-city military subcommand, a branch of the provincial military command, so they obtained some handguns, rifles, machine guns, hand grenades, etc. After that, the fighting became more violent and deadly. Facing the worsening situation, the leaders of our Regiment ordered the attached factory to make spears for all members. One day, we were notified that the spears would be distributed to each of us. The spear was made of a sharp head and welded to a six-foot-long steel pipe. I never dreamed that as an engineering student, I would be given such an ancient weapon.

Instead of attacking with the pen, some organizations started to launch military assaults upon each other. Now the "Cultural" Revolution was turned into the true warfare. Fortunately, our campus had not been attacked until the end of June.

Morning, June 30, 1967, I was awakened up by noises in our dormitory.

"Get up and gather at the front door of the dormitory! Our college has been surrounded by our opponents!" The team leader shouted.

Quickly we got up and ran to the front door.

"The Regiment leaders ordered that we are to defend the east gate," the team leader said, "Now, go to prepare yourselves for the battle, we must drive them away!"

During the preparation somebody made a creative use of our textbooks, which were all paperback of the letter size, and the thicknesses were from a half inch to one inch. Two textbooks were put in front and back of our torso to protect hearts, and two on each side to protect our kidneys. The books were fixed in place by the leather belt to form an armor, then covered by a jacket. This invention was quickly adopted by all of us.

Holding the spears and with textbook-made armors, we went to the battle field.

One of our classmates who was a trumpet player in the college's brass band, now acted as a bugle player using his instrument. When the trumpet sounded the PLA charge signal, which we heard many times in war movies, the east gate was opened. We all shouted "comrades, charge!" –Just like the PLA soldiers in movies –and then rushed out of the gate. After running out, I saw a couple of our opponents throwing some objects from the other side of the road. Then I heard an explosion. Somebody on my right, behind me, immediately cried "Ah, my leg!" I turned my head and saw a student falling to the ground with both hands holding his right knee. I recognized him as the pentathlon champion of our college annual sports games. Two fellow students ran to him with a stretcher. I helped the two to move the champion onto the stretcher, and saw that his face had turned pale and

Living in Mao's Era

his pants were soaked with blood. The strong blood smell made me sick. He was then carried away for medical treatment.

Since our people far outnumbered our opponents, the opponents quickly escaped. The bugle sounded to call off the battle. We returned to our school, and closed the east gate. Then we went to the student dining hall to have our breakfast. During the breakfast, I learned that the battle at the school's main entrance on the west side was far more violent. Mr. *Lu*, a freshman in the Department of Mining and Mineral Processing, was shot in the forehead by a small caliber rifle, and died with his eyes wide open. Also, many more students were injured there.

After breakfast, we were ordered to retreat to inside the city where the vast majority of people were on our side. Our team was to defend the west city gate. G-city was initially established in the *Qin* Dynasty, more than two thousand years ago. Like all cities of the ancient times, G-city used to have a city wall with four gates. Most parts of the city wall had been taken away for new constructions, so was the west gate. There was no wall or gate at that place any more, but the name was still used to designate the location.

City residents brought us food and water for lunch and supper. Nothing happened during the day. And there were no further instructions from the top of our organization. In the evening, our team had a meeting to discuss what to do next. One said that our opponents were supported by the district PLA unit which gave modern weaponry to them. But we had only spears. There would be no chance for us to win the battle. Everybody agreed. It seemed that we should retreat. But another student said we were supposed to defend the Chairman Mao's revolutionary line with our lives and blood, how could we retreat? Facing this dilemma, we were all falling into silence.

Finally, one broke the silence:

> "It is true that we are all loyal to Chairman Mao, but it does not mean we all must die here. Chairman Mao teaches us: 'Human beings are the most valuable in the world. And as long as we have people, any miracle can be created.' We all know that after the fifth anti-siege failed in the early 1930s, Chairman Mao led the famous long march. This was to preserve the revolutionary seeds. In the current situation,

I think we must follow Chairman Mao's approach, and preserve our lives to better service our motherland. If we all die, it is not just the loss of our personal lives, but also a loss to Chairman Mao, a loss to the revolutionary masses, and the loss to our dear motherland."

What an eloquent and brilliant argument! Nobody raised a further question. We decided to break up into smaller groups, and separately find some residents who were willing to protect us, so that we would not die at the same time.

For the same reason, I asked my sister to go separately because it was less likely for both of us to be caught when we hid in different places.

The city residents were very supportive. Four other students and I quickly found a house where all the residents would be willing to protect us. This was an old-fashioned two-story wooden house, which had two side rooms, occupied by two families, and a big central hall shared by the two families as their living and dining room. There was attic above the ceiling of the central hall, with a small opening at one corner. A ladder was used to climb up and down the attic. The residents proposed that we hide in this attic. After we climbed into the attic, they could move away the ladder. This made the attic an ideal place to hide. A wood-made portable toilet was put into the attic for us. A big porcelain tea pot with drinking water was also provided. In case we needed help, we could knock on the ceiling. Twice a day, they would use a bamboo stick to knock on the ceiling, telling us it was safe to come down for a meal.

The attic had not been used for years and was very dusty. There was no window and no light. In July it was very hot. The temperature in the attic could reach 100-degree Fahrenheit in the afternoon, and the attic was like a hell. To avoid being noticed, we tried not to utter any sound. We could hear machine gun firing here and there. From time to time we could also hear explosions. Thinking about the injured champion, and with the bloody scene still fresh in my mind, I could not fall asleep. I was utterly bewildered about why people acted as if they all had lost their minds?

After hiding in the attic for a couple of days, we noticed that the sounds of the gunshots went down. The opponent organizations started to search. One morning, a group came in. They searched two side houses and did not find anybody. One of them asked a little girl in the hall:

"Is there anybody in the attic?"

Hearing this, my heart almost jumped to my throat. Except praying, there was nothing else I could do.

The little girl answered calmly: "No. The attic was extremely dirty. Nobody climbed there for a very long time."

The group went away. We all appreciate the girl's quick wit and serene manner.

After the search team was gone, our hosts thought it was safe to come down for a meal. Just when we came down and finished washing, one of the residents hurried in and said another searching team was coming. There was no time to climb back to the attic, so we were all caught. First, we were blindfolded with a piece of black cloth. Then a rope was used to tie five of us up. After that we were led out of this house.

Although being blindfolded, I was able to see through the fabric. It was sunny, but rarely was there anybody in the street. Sometimes, I could see the similar groups of blindfolded captives walking in the various directions. They were caught by different organizations of our opponents. Finally, we entered the yard of a government office building. Then we were led into their dining hall, and were asked to sit on a long bench. At that time, they removed the fabrics that covered our eyes. We saw the hall were full of people, and most of them were young students, because most students were on our side. I recognized many of them were from our college.

After a short while, a middle-aged officer walked to us, and asked us to write a self-criticizing document, acknowledging that we made mistakes. We were allowed to write just one for the five of us, and sign our names together. We discussed the situation and believed that at that time, we lost this round of struggle to our opponents. However, it did not mean our faction was ultimately lost. The situation could reverse in the future. To avoid this self-criticizing document being used to against us later, like *Qu Qiubai's* "Redundant Words," we carefully worded this document. We emphasized that we were following Chairman Mao's call to take part in the Cultural Revolution. We might not understand Chairman Mao's Supreme Directives fully, or might not implement them well, so some mistakes could have been made, but we had never intentionally made those mistakes. We were now determined to study Chairman Mao's books more diligently, as well as the editorials of "Two Newspapers and One Magazine," and the related instructions issued by the Party, and to continue with the Cultural Resolution until its eventual victory."

When the officer came again, we gave the document to him, fearing that he might not let us pass easily in this first round of self-criticism, as it usually was the case. However, he just took over our document, and added to the stack of documents written by others, without even looking at it. Then he told us: "Go to the other end of this dining hall, take your free meals, and then you can go back to your school." We breathed a huge relief, thinking we were lucky. Later we learned that in early July, there had been an airplane circling around G-city spreading circulars titled "The provincial military command's order to stop fighting in G-city." The officers working in the government organizations were more sensitive to the Party's policies, so they acted more cautiously and gently. It was said that captives caught by some other organizations were beaten and sent to the countryside as punishment.

When we were back, we found that the campus was unusually quiet. There was no sign that our campus was invaded, and our personal belongs in the dormitory were intact. We did not see a lot of students, like the days before this battle. But we had no energy to find out the details. After several days of irregular meals and sleeps, we were all exhausted, and wanted to lie on our own beds to have a good sleep.

Next morning, I went to the sports field for morning jogging and saw Professor *Li*. Seeing each other we were both excited.

"You are still alive!" We both uttered the same words.

Prof. *Li* told me that he had been hiding in the attic of our physics laboratory and brought two pumpkins with him.

"How did you cook the pumpkins?" I asked.

"Cooking? I ate them raw!"

"How does the raw pumpkin taste?"

"Well, when one is hungry, any food is delicious!"

Gradually, more and more students returned. Each one had some adventurous story. When our classmate Mr. *Xu* returned, at first, we did not even recognize him. He wore old patched clothes, and his skin was suntanned to dark brown. With his baring feet and worn out bamboo hat, he looked just like a typical fisherman. As it turned out, he indeed hid in a fisherman's boat during that time. He traded his good shirt, jacket, dress pant, socks, and sneakers for the fisherman's old worn clothes. In the past few days, he voluntarily helped with fishing. In return, he would share the fisherman's food, and was given a spot to sleep on the boat. With such a genuine costume, he could hardly be recognized as a college student, and nobody paid attention to him. When selling his fish inside the city, the fisherman got a copy of the circular "The provincial military command's order to stop fighting in G-city." Mr. *Xu* read the circular and knew it was safe to return.

He told me that from the fishing boat he saw my sister and another girl walking across the nearby bridge in early July. Hearing this, I felt a great relief: my sister was fine after the battle. But a few days later, she was back to our college. She told me that when she and another girl walked to the other end of the bridge, they were stopped by somebody in the opponent organization because they looked like students, and most students were on our side. As a result, they were detained. But they were released shortly when the provincial military command's order became widely known.

On July 12, a PLA division was ordered to enter G-city to protect and support our faction. More than 100 military trucks drove through the streets. Hearing the news we were all excited and ran out to welcome them. Watching the trucks slowly drove by the boulevard outside our main campus, all onlookers shouted enthusiastically:

"Learn from the PLA!"

"Salute the PLA!"

"Long live the PLA!"

"Long live Chairman Mao's Proletarian Revolution Line!"

"Long, long, long live Chairman Mao!"

After this parade, a company of the PLA troop was garrisoned in our college. This made us feel much safer. The PLA unit played a great role in restoring the order and stabilizing the situation. In addition, the PLA troop also provided excellent medical and other services.

With the PLA's support, our lives were back to normal. The shops and restaurants were back to normal, the post office was also reopened. My sister and I went to the post office to send a telegram to Mama telling her that we were both safe and fine.

A few days later, my sister and another female student went to Beijing to report the situation in G-city to the Mass Reception Stations of the CCRG.

Mama later told me that upon receiving our telegram, she immediately kneeled and prayed to thank Jesus for protecting us. She also told me that in one school in N-city, there was a small group of students from our college. They published the names of the casualties of our college on a daily basis, during the fighting days. When some parents saw their children's names on the list, they would break into tears, and some even passed out. For those, who did not see their children's names on the list, would anxiously come again the next day. Some parents became friends when they exchanged their children's information and learned that their children were classmates.

About a month later, an exhibition opened on the first floor in the building of the Department of Mining and Mineral Processing. It was for mourning the martyrs killed during the battles between the two factions. When entering the main entrance of the building, the hall was decorated like a funeral house, with white paper flowers[73] and wreaths. The funereal music was also repeatedly played at low volume. In the classrooms, many photos were shown the cruelty of how captives were treated by the opposing organizations.

One classroom was for displaying the martyrs of our college, total 26 of them, several of them I knew personally:

> Mr. *Sun*, the chief commander of our East Red Regiment, was killed by a grenade in a battle. He had retreated to an empty house and later surrounded by the opponents. Before he died, he tore a corner of a poster on the wall, about palm-size, and wrote down his last words: "Dear comrades, I strongly believe that Chairman Mao's Proletarian Revolutionary Line would win its victory eventually. I am going to fight for it until my last drop of

---

[73]   In China, white flowers are for funerals, red flowers are for weddings.

blood. This is my last goodbye to all my comrade-in-arms of the East Red Regiment! Long live Chairman Mao!"

Mr. *Zhong* was graduated in 1965 and assigned the job as a faculty member of our Department. He was a member of the communist party and used to be the chairman of the college student union for several years. He was killed in the G-city Paper Manufacturing Plant. His body was thrown into their plant's acid pool and dissolved, according to the description.

Mr. Wu, who graduated from the Sixth High School of N-city and came to the college with me on the same bus in 1962, and had also hid in an attic of a local resident. When the opponent's search team was in the house, one of them fired a round into the attic, hitting him in the stomach. But he dared not utter any sound, fearing the opponents would discover him and a couple of other students hidden there. Unfortunately, his blood dropped through the bullet holes, and he was exposed together with the others. The opponents climbed into the attic, and ordered all of them to climb down. Those who were not injured were able to climb down. But the injured Mr. *Wu* was too weak to move. Then the opponents threw him down and he died immediately. A photo showed that his blood splashed onto the wall.

In other exhibition rooms, there were photos of the corpses of the martyrs that were hurriedly buried after they were executed, and some of them with both hands bound with steel wires. I could have been one of them, had I been caught by some barbarian group of our opponents. The corpses were dug out for reburial as revolutionary heroes soon after the PLA troop arrived.

In October 1967, the CPC Central Committee, the CCRG, the State Council, and the Central Committee of the CPC Military Commission issued a joint notice "Revolution by Resuming Classes for Students of Colleges, Middle Schools, and Elementary Schools."

Finally, the fighting nightmare in our city came to an end, and we were back to what the student should have been doing: studying.

After discussing with our professors, we decided to go to Shanghai to continue our graduation practice. We went to the Third Steel of Shanghai, but there was no progress made in continuous casting. We were disappointed. Then, we learned that the students who were to graduate in summer of 1966 were to graduate and to be assigned jobs soon. After the 1966-year college students graduated, our turn would come next. So, there might not be enough time to work on the detailed graduation project. We thought perhaps it was better to just visit various steel companies and research institutions to gain broader knowledge about the status of the steel industry, and this was what we did. The practice in Shanghai lasted about two months until near the Chinese New Year. Then we went home and waited for notification of our graduation.

I went back to N-city to spend the Chinese New Year with Mama. After the holidays, we did not hear any news about the time of our graduation. The classmates whose family were in N-city just continued to stay home, rather than going back to our campus.

Just like in G-city, there was chaotic fighting in N-city and other parts of J-province. The PLA troop, led by political commissar *Sheng* was dispatched to J-province to stabilize the situation. Upon arriving, Commissar *Sheng* reorganized the provincial military command and supported the rebelling faction of the mass organization.

On the other hand, the F-Prefectural military command in the northeast of J-province supported the opponents. The fighting between the mass organizations eventually dragged in their supporting PLA units. The fighting became a real military combat. According to some eyewitnesses, they saw some unbelievable scenes where the soldiers wearing PLA uniforms were firing at each other because they supported different organizations. They had to wear armbands to distinguish each other.

Many students, who determined to defend Chairman's Revolution Line with their flesh and blood, followed the PLA troop into the battle field. Without military training, those brave young students easily shed their blood or became martyrs.

Finally, the side supported by the Prefectural military command, together with its supporting Prefectural troop, was defeated.

In China, the *Qingming* festival, which is in early April, and is the traditional day to commemorate ancestors and to mourn dead family members, relatives, and friends. During that day, people would go to the cemetery to clean the tombs of their loved ones, burn incense and fake paper money, etc.

In the 1968 *Qingming* festival, a couple of my classmates proposed that we visit the cemetery in the north suburb of N-city. When getting there, we first visited the memorial hall, where we saw shelves neatly placed like the bookshelves in a library. Each shelf had many cinerary caskets, and on their front sides there was a photo of the deceased.

Dozens of shelves were dedicated to the youngsters who had sacrificed their lives for Chairman Mao's Revolutionary Line, most of them aged only14 to16. After reading the notes on the front of the caskets, we learned that these boys and girls were killed in the battle on August 24, 1967, during the F-Prefecture battle mentioned above.

In May 1968 another political campaign, "Cleaning Class Ranks" started. In addition to the old Black Types, three new black types were added during the early stage of the Cultural Revolution: the traitor, the spy, and the capitalist roader. And, now two more categories were added: the might-have-been-rightists who slipped through the "net" in 1957, and dregs of the KMT. General *Sheng* gave the campaign some additional tasks: "Three Searches:" search for traitors, search for spies, and search for active counter-revolutionists. The "Dregs of the KMT" were interpreted by some as anyone who worked in the cities before the Liberation.

One day, a neighbor told us a horrifying story. An engineer, worked in the power generation station near the river, committed suicide by jumping into the river, because he worked at the power station before the Liberation, and was regarded as a dreg of KMT. As mentioned before, any suicide was regarded as counter-revolutionary, his action would put his family into the Black category. His wife felt there would be no future for them, based on their life experience at that time. Under the double attacks of the grief of losing a loved one and the associated political consequence, the wife and two kids killed themselves by wrapping electric wires on them. Fearing the youngest kid might be afraid and cry, which would screw up their suicide plan, the wife and the elder son put a handkerchief into the younger kid's mouth before they turned on the electricity.

Years later, I read an article by *Hu Ping*, a university Professor. The article revealed the horror of the Cleaning Class Ranks Campaign In J-province. General *Sheng* announced that J-province would blow a Red Hurricane to wipe out the class enemies. According to the article, in one office, a denounced man used a pair of scissors to open his belly, shouting in the hallway:

"Everyone look by your eyes and see whether my heart is red or black!"

General *Sheng* allowed the masses, i.e. the ordinary people, to arrest and execute class enemies without going through the judicial system. It was like another wave of red terror.

Hearing some rumors that we would graduate soon, we returned to our campus. During our absence, the monument for martyrs of the Cultural Revolution of our college was erected on the main campus. The photos of the 26 martyrs were painted on white ceramic tiles with a few lines to describe their lives, and then cemented around the middle of the monument. Big gold-plated letters, in Mao's calligraphic style, "Revolutionary Martyrs Are Immortal" were inscribed on the monument, above those photos.

Soon after we returned, the CPC Central Committee, the CCRG, the State Council, and the Central Committee of the CPC Military Commission issued a joint notice about Job Assignment for the 1967 college graduates. The notice proposed the principle of going to the factories and the mines, going to the rural areas and the countryside, going to the board areas, and going to the grass-roots units, for the job assignment. This principle was also called "*Si Ge Mian Xiang*" (Four Goings) for short.

In our job assignment plan, five would be assigned to the army farm, and the rest would go to factories and the military construction unit. In the past, the job assigning was done by college and department leaders. But due to the Cultural Revolution, the old college and department leaders were still sidelined at the time of our graduation. A temporary job assigning group was set up, consisting of some professors and department officers who were also the member of the East Red Regiment, the leaders of our class, which was called "combat team," in the East Red Regiment.

It was understandable that nobody liked to go to the army farm because we were engineering major and could not gain any relevant experience working on farmland. But the quota must be fulfilled, and somebodies must go. Instead of persuasion, the job assigning group adopted a class struggle approach. There happened to have such an opportunity for their strategy.

One of our classmates, Mr. *Xu*, had his family background classified as the Middle Peasant class during the 1950 Agrarian Reform. But in 1960, it had been reclassified to the Rich Peasant class. Thinking this was unfair, he filed an appeal to the people's commune of his village. His letter was handed over to our leaders by the people's commune. The job assigning group made use of this incident, alleged that Mr. *Xu* was not able to make a clear line of demarcation from his exploitive parents, and stood on the side of his exploitive parents. A series of meetings were organized to denounce him about his serious political mistake. Most students in my class had Black family backgrounds due to the family background check was the most lenient in 1962. By striking Mr. *Xu*, most of us would be intimidated and would obey their decisions. And after Mr. *Xu* was crushed, the job assigning group started naming the other four students that they wanted to send to the army farm by revealing their family backgrounds and problematic Social Relationships. I was one of them. Once these difficult assignments were done, the others were relatively easy.

Among other job positions, there were two to work in Shanghai. One was in the Second Steel of Shanghai, the other was in the Machine Repairing Corporation of Shanghai. One classmate, Mr. *Hong*, was diagnosed with tuberculosis just before the graduation. He was assigned to work in the Second Shanghai Steel because the hospitals in Shanghai were top-rated. Another position could have been given to Miss *Chang*, whose fiancé was working in Shanghai. But the job assigning group thought Miss *Chang* was from the Landlord family, and could not be treated kindly. She was assigned to the L-Steel Company in H-province. Based on the Chinese *Hukou* (residence registration) policy, it was extremely difficult, if not impossible, for a spouse to move from small cities to large cities. This assignment would guarantee that Miss *Chang*'s spouse would have to leave Shanghai, if they wanted to live together. Even so, the transfer process was time-consuming.

The position of the Machine Repairing Corporation of Shanghai was assigned to Mr. *Xi, who* was a single. The job assigning group explained the rationale in their decision as follows.

Due to the historical reasons, Shanghai, which was called the Paradise of Adventurers in the past, was regarded as the most bourgeois city in China. Mr. *Xi* was from a Poor Peasant family, which was one of the Red Types, and was *"Gen Zhen Miao Hong* (decent root with red sprout). Therefore, he would be able to resist the bourgeois influence in Shanghai, and would not be spoiled. Moreover, during his years in the college, Mr. *Xi* had demonstrated his proletarian stand by keeping his rustic lifestyle, and rarely interacted with female students. This had demonstrated his firm proletarian stand.

As it turned out two years later, these job assignments were inconvenient for Miss *Chang* and a tragedy for Mr. *Xi.*

Job change in China was not easy, even in a move from a large city to a small city. During Mao's era, all employees in the cities were assigned jobs and paid by the central government. If one moved out, the unit he or she worked was not authorized to hire a replacement immediately. Instead, the unit must file a request and wait for the central government to send a person, who either was approved to transfer to this unit from another unit, or was a new college graduate. During that waiting period, the rest of the employees would have to work harder to finish the unit's assigned tasks by the central government.

On the other hand, all the employees were paid by the government, not by any specific organization. There was no financial burden to organizations if they had more employees. Consequently, organization leaders were generally reluctant to let anybody leave.

In addition, there were tedious procedures associated with moving from one city to another, such as moving their residence registrations, which was handled by the public security system. So, after her marriage, Miss. *Chang* and her husband lived separately for some years before her husband left Shanghai and joined her in H-province.

Mr. *Xi* was even more unfortunate. In March 1970 when I returned from the army farm, I stopped by Shanghai to see the two classmates working there. Mr. *Hong* met me at the train station and told me what happened to Mr. *Xi.* A girl working in his group approached him, probably because he was the only single male with a college degree in this group. But he was too shy to express himself. The girl mistook it, thinking he was arrogant, and might not be interested in her —at that time men were supposed to actively court girls. Actually, he loved that girl very much. So, he sought help from Mr. *Hong*, another classmate, and told him that he thought about this girl even in dreams. Mr. *Hong* helped him by accompanying Mr. *Xi* to visit the girl in her home. The girl was glad to see Mr. *Xi* and warmly welcomed them. However, during their stay, Mr. *Xi* did not say very much, "he just sat there like a statue!" Mr. *Hong* told me. To make the atmosphere more relaxed, Mr. *Hong* tried his best to keep talking and telling jokes.

Near lunch time, Mr. *Xi* stood up and wanted to leave, because it was a custom that unless invited in advance, one was not supposed to stay for meals as guests. But the girl and her mother warmly welcomed them both to have lunch together. Mr. *Hong* winked at Mr. *Xi* repeatedly, urging him to stay. It was not clear why Mr. *Xi* insisted on leaving, but they did. This made the matter worse, as the girl felt she was losing face and offended. From then on, the girl did not even look at Mr. *Xi*. He became depressed, and started behaving strangely. For example, his dormitory roommates saw him opening his umbrella inside his mosquito net several times. Concerned, the roommates reported this to the corporate leaders, and he ended up in a mental hospital.

Hearing this sad story, I asked Mr. *Hong* to accompany me to see Mr. *Xi*. After the treatment, he was better and could recognize me. We chatted briefly. Among his treatment was electric shock. He told me that this treatment was like the electric torture in movies. Later, when he was discharged from the hospital, his elder sister asked the leaders of the Machine Repairing Corporation of Shanghai to allow Mr. *Xi* to move from Shanghai to his home town. As a result, this precious job position in Shanghai was not only wasted, but also had tragic consequences.

In the past, there had been a graduation banquet every year, and we were looking forward to ours. However, somebody proposed that instead of a banquet as before, it made more revolutionary sense to eat an ideologically correct meal, consisting of the red rice and the pumpkin soup, the main food of Chairman Mao and his comrades in the famous red base of *Jinggang* Mountain in the late 1920s.

So, trucks were dispatched to the revolutionary holy place to buy the genuine *Jinggang* red rice and pumpkins for our culturally revolutionary graduation-meal. Despite being disappointed, I still felt lucky that nobody had proposed to eat so-called *Yi Ku Fan*, or remembering bitterness meal.

The so-called *Yi Ku Fan* was essentially like hogwash, which was said to be the main food for poor people before the Liberation. We had eaten this several times, as a part of the class struggle education. The rationale of eating a *Yi Ku* meal was that by eating such meal, we would be reminded that comparing to the time before the Liberation, we were much happier now due to the great leadership of the Party, and should appreciate it.

Near the end of July, 1968, a dramatic event occurred. The Worker's Mao Zedong Thought propaganda Team entered Tsinghua University, to stop the fighting between two factions there. During this process, one faction resisted fiercely and caused the death and injury of members of the propaganda team. As a gesture of support, in early August, Chairman Mao sent mangos, which had been a gift to Chairman Mao, given by the foreign minister of Pakistan, to the Beijing Worker's Mao Zedong Thought propaganda Team. This was the headline news of all newspapers. The mango was very rare in China at that time, pictures of the yellow colored fruit were also shown in the newspaper.

A few weeks later, the well-known editorial of People's Daily, "Working Class Should Lead Everything," was published. This editorial was a milestone which effectively announced the end of the era that young students were the pioneers of the Cultural Revolution. Before that editorial, young students, mainly middle and high school students, were always praised as *Ge Ming Xiao Jiang* (little revolutionary generals). After that, young students obtained a new collective name *Zhi Shi Qing Nian* (Educated Youth), and they were advised to be "re-educated" by the workers, and the Poor and Lower-Middle class peasants.

In the following *Shang Shan Xia Xiang* (going to the mountain area and the countryside), they were to become farmers, far away from their homes. My sister, who was in the second year of her vocational school when the Cultural Revolution started in 1966, was sent to *Sheng Xin* farm near N-city, as an Educated Youth.

It was very interesting to learn how the mangos, the Chairman's gift to the Working Class, were eaten.

Due to the limited quantity, each factory, some of which had thousands of workers, received only one piece. To let all workers enjoy the gift from Chairman Mao, the factory leaders decided to cut the mango into pieces and put them into several big woks filled with water. When the water boiled, the workers would line up with their cups. Each worker would receive one ladle of the mango soup. In the late 1970s, I got a chance to visit one textile factory in the east of Beijing. In the lobby, pictures were put into their display window to show the cooking process, and the lines of pious workers waiting for their turn to receive this priceless soup.

Army Farm (1968-1970)

Those, who assigned to go to the Army Farm in our college, were required to report to the PLA stationed at YK-city of L-Province in early September. I stayed with Mama in N-city for a month, then left for army farm by train. On my way, I stopped in Beijing for a couple of days to see my younger brother and my uncle's family.

My uncle was still locked up in a "cowshed" and not allowed to see any family member or relative. I was only able to see my aunt, and with her beloved husband still locked in "cowshed," her mood was quite melancholy. When waving goodbye to me, she started to weep, uncontrollably. This was the last time I saw her. She passed away three months later and my uncle was allowed to bid a final farewell to his wife of more than thirty years, before her body was cremated.

Arriving at YK-city railroad station, I noticed a reception station with a big sign "Welcome College Graduates" had been set up there by the military unit. I handed in my document and registered there. A dozen graduates from the Beijing Institute of Iron and Steel had arrived before me. After we got our check-in baggage. A military truck carried us to the PLA barracks in the city. A few days later, we were transferred to the Army Farm in P-area by boat.

The Army Farm was situated near the west coast of the *Liao Dong* Bay in the *Bohai* Sea. In the places where I had previously lived, there were always some mountains or hills in sight. This Army Farm area was quite flat, and this scene made me recall the folk song of nomadic tribes that describe the grasslands:

> By the foot of the *Ying* Mountain,
> The *Chile* prairie is situated.

The dome-like sky
Covers over the earth.
The sky is blue.
The wild is boundless.
Cattle and Sheep only appear,
When the wind bends the grass lowers

The college graduates assigned to this Army Farm were from four colleges: the Beijing Institute of Iron and Steel, the Middle-South Institute of Mining and Metallurgy, the *Kunming* Institute of Engineering, and our college. These four colleges were financially supported by the Ministry of Metallurgy and educationally managed by the Ministry of Education. Soon after I reported to the Army Farm, the graduates from the first two colleges were also reported to the military unit. While waiting for the graduates from the *Kunming* Institute of Engineering, we started building additional houses.

First, we need to fetch some reed for the roof, and the reed growing area was about one hour walking. Scythes were used to cut the reeds, and then we tied the reeds into bundles and carried them back on our backs. After getting enough reeds, we started the construction work. The layouts of houses were marked by the local professional workers, with lime powder.

Like the traditional house in the northern China, our houses were faced the south, and the windows and doors were all on the southern side, to make good use of the sun. The main entrance of the house was in the middle of the south wall. Outside the door, there was a small room with a door opening to the east side. The purpose of this small room was to prevent the wind from blowing directly into the main entrance in the cold winter.

Inside the main door was the middle room, used as the dining area. On each side of the middle room, there was a sleeping room. There was a door for each sleeping room. Each sleeping room had a passageway and one *Kang*[74] on each side of it. In the middle room, there was one straw burning

---

[74] In north China, the bed was built with bricks, which has smoke passages inside, and the passages were connected to a Chimney. In winter, firewood or other fuels were used to heat up such a bed.

stove with big cast iron wok on each side, to make hot water for washing, and also to heat the *Kang* for each sleeping room.

We first mixed the mud with the straw, which was cut into pieces about two inches long. Then we used garden forks to put the mixture along the lime marked lines, about two feet in thickness. In this way, the mud mixture was stacked layer by layer until the wall reached the designed height. Some window and door frames were added in certain places when we worked on the walls. Then the local workers would put the wood roof frames on the wall and added the reeds on the frame. Finally, we added another layer of the mud mixture on the top of reeds to finish up the roof. The windows were covered with thick translucent plastic sheets. We built three additional houses this way.

Shortly after we finished building the houses, the graduates from the *Kunming* Institute of Engineering arrived. Then we were organized into military units. The graduates from the four colleges were mixed and organized into three companies, which formed one battalion. Each company had its own camp, and consisted of four platoons. The male graduates formed the first three platoons, and the female graduates formed the fourth platoon. The lieutenant colonel, the battalion political commissar, the captain, the deputy captain, the company political instructor, the quartermaster, and the lieutenants were the corresponding military officers from the PLA. The deputy lieutenant and all sergeants were the college graduates appointed by the PLA leaders. Under the quartermaster, there was a cook-house squad, comprised of all college graduates, responsible for cooking meals for the whole company. I was assigned to the first squad of the second platoon in the third company. Our lieutenant, a PLA lieutenant, was from S-province. The deputy lieutenant, our sergeant, and most of the graduates in my squad were from the Middle-South Institute of Mining and Metallurgy.

Three of my college classmates, who were also assigned to the Army Farm, were in the first company, and Mr. *Xu* was in the second company. Our camps were separated by about 15 minutes walking distance.

Our daily life started at 6:00 a.m. when a bugle gave the signal for getting up. In half an hour, we started the morning ritual. First, we all would recite 2-3 Chairman Mao's quotations, or supreme directives, from the famous small "red book," then we all would face the east, the direction of the rising sun, to perform the Loyalty Dance, which we learned when we arrived.

The dance music was a *XinJiang* folk song. The preparatory gesture was to bend the right knee a little, to slightly lower our body, and put two hands at the heart position, with the right hand holding Mao's little red book. When the music started, we'd straighten the right leg to raise our bodies, singing the lyrics "dear Chairman Mao," and at the same time, throw our two hands towards the sun, to express that we'd submit our loyal hearts to Chairman Mao...

After that, we'd run around the camp for 30 minutes, and, from time to time, shouting "1-2-3-4" in unison with our steps.

Then we'd eat breakfast.

After our breakfast, we'd start to work in the field starting at 8:00 a.m. There was a one-hour lunch break at noon. Most of the time, we'd have a one hour nap, after lunch. Then we'd continue working in the field until 5:30 p.m.

After dinner, we'd have political study starting at 7:00 p.m. During that time, we'd study editorials from "Two Newspaper and One Magazine." Normally we'd take turn to read loudly of those editorials, and then we'd discuss the important messages in those articles. If there was no important editorial, we'd read Mao's "Selected Works." We were required to apply the ideas we learned from the articles and Mao's books to our daily activities. The evening session ended at 9:30 p.m. and the light would be turned off at 10:00 p.m.

On Sunday, we were allowed to leave our barracks from 8 a.m. to 5 p.m. We must orally apply for the leave before we left, and report to our lieutenant again when we were back.

Soon came the harvest time. Before we came, there had been a PLA unit to grow rice here. Now the ripe rice waved with the wind and made the field look like a huge golden lake. Since the time we were in middle schools, we had helped the peasants during the harvesting season, so we all knew how to use the sickle. All the PLA officers would work together with us, and they all had very good agricultural skills. During the laboring, we were encouraged to sing songs. The PLA officers also chat with us. Soon we were friends. The rice was cut and stacked on the threshing ground. It must be put there for several weeks before the rice can be threshed.

In the chat during our harvesting, I learned a lot of interesting things from graduates from other colleges. There was a rumor in 1966 that the students in the Middle-South Institute of Mining and Metallurgy stormed the student archive department to search for so-called "black materials" in their dossiers, because it was said that those dossiers mainly contain negative information about people.

Since the majority of graduates in my platoon were from this college, out of curiosity, I asked them about this event. They confirmed that it indeed happened. Some students stormed the archive department and looked at their own dossiers. They angrily burned those dossiers,[75] because the dossiers were indeed mainly contained negative facts and comments about them.

They also confirmed that in each dossier, there was the stamp of the conclusion of the family background check, made by the public security department. These dossiers were regarded as the top national secret, and nobody in China would be allowed to look at their own dossiers.

It was said that this system was copied from the Soviet Union.

In my squad, there were two graduates from the Beijing Institute of Iron and Steel. Most universities in Beijing are located in *Haidian* district, and close to each other. So I asked them whether they heard about a student at Tsinghua University named *Xu Gongsheng*.

"Ah! He is famous!" One answered, "How do you know him?"

"He is my high school classmate," I answered.

"He was a fencing champion of Beijing universities. But he died in the so-called "One Hundred Day Fighting" between two factions in the Tsinghua University during the Cultural Revolution."

I was astonished, and asked how this could happen at such a famous university in Beijing.

"Since he had good fencing skills, he injured several students in the opposite faction. So, in one battle, he was isolated and surrounded by more than a dozen of the opponents. He was able to fight and retreat backwardly. But, unfortunately there was a small shallow hole on his way back, he stepped into it and fell down. Those opponents took this

---

[75] It was said that the dossiers were re-established later.

opportunity to stab him on his legs, then left. When his comrades came back a while later and carried the unconscious champion to a hospital, he had lost too much blood, and the doctors were not able to revive him."

We fell into silence for a while and then ended our conversation with a deep sigh.

Once a graduate in our platoon was sick. Another graduate wearing thick black-framed glasses walked in to see him. Pulling out some needles from his plastic box and sterilizing them, he started to perform acupuncture to this sick comrade. After he finished, this comrade felt much better. Then he left.

Amazing about his medical skills, I was curious about him. As it turned out he was from the Middle-South Institute of Mining and Metallurgy, and in the third platoon. In my squad, there were a couple of fellows from this institute, so I turned to them for more information.

I was told that he was from a village near C-city where the college was located. One day during the early stages of the Cultural Revolution in 1966, a peasant from this home village came to the college and reported an urgent news to him: his whole family had been detained and was to be executed with other landlords and rich peasant families, because in early 1950s, his father was classified as the Landlord. The local association of the Poor and Lower-Middle peasants decided to purify their village by eliminating all the class enemies and their family members.

He hurried back to the village and begged for sparing his younger brothers and sisters. He defended his brothers and sisters by saying that they were born after the Liberation and had nothing to do with their old family business.

He learned acupuncture from an old Chinese medical doctor when he was in high school in a nearby town. Over the years he volunteered to use his acupuncture skills to cure common illness of many villagers, including the head of the Poor and Lower-Middle Peasant Association. The head granted leniency to his younger brothers and sisters. But his father and mother were killed together with other class enemies and their families.

Upon hearing his story, I felt strong compassion toward this poor guy: such a horrendous memory would accompany him for the rest of his life!

During the holidays, we followed the tradition of northern China to eat *Jiao-zi* (dumping). On October 1, the national day, the cook-house squad prepared doughs, threaded meat and chopped celery cabbages for us to make dumplings. But most of us in the second platoon were from south of China and did not know how to make dumplings. So, we decided to make pancakes using those materials. When we were making the pancakes, Mr. *Zhang,* our deputy captain walked in.

"What are you doing?" He appeared puzzled.

"Meat Pancake." Someone answered with embarrassment.

"You don't like *Jiao zi*?"

"..."

"Ah! You are from south, and probably don't know how to make *Jiao zi*, right?" He smiled and continued: *"Jiao zi* is so delicious, I think you would like to learn this skill, don't you?"

"Of course!" We answered.

"Let me teach you. This skill could be a good souvenir that you learned in our PLA Army Farm."

He demonstrated the whole process from preparing the wrapper to wrapping up a perfect *Jiao Zi*. Then he watched us practice it, and correct our wrong actions until we could make reasonably good dumplings.

Indeed, from then on, each time when I make dumping at home, I would remember our deputy captain's comments, his smiling face, and the scene he taught us this wonderful cooking skill.

After living in the army farm for several months, we found that there was a significant management difference between the PLA and the civilian organizations. In civilian organizations, people were frequently criticized or even denounced for various problems. In the PLA, praise and encouragement were dominantly used, and no single college student was publicly criticized. Each week, someone was elected as the "Good Comrade" whose merits were praised and other people were encouraged to learn from this good comrade. As a result, the relations among comrades-in-arms were much friendlier.

In such an environment, we felt much more relaxed in the army farm than in civilian organizations.

From time to time, we would gather in the open space of the battalion headquarters to watch open-air movies. Cross-legged, we seated ourselves on the ground. Due to the Cultural Revolution, many movies were regarded as problematic. In addition to newsreels, only several old movies produced in the early 1950s and the Soviet movie "Lenin in October" were shown many times. Because the repetition, we all could recite the dialogues, and some could even imitate the gestures and expressions vividly.

At other times, the Mao Zedong Thought Propaganda teams from nearby factories or schools would come to perform dances and singing. Once, there was a Mao Zedong Thought Propaganda Team consisting of the dumb and deaf children. Their performances were mainly reciting Chairman Mao's Quotations, Royal Dances, and simple songs. We were told that those children were cured by acupuncture.

During the Cultural Revolution, Chairman Mao's quotation –"Chinese medicine is a great treasure house, it should be diligently dug and developed"—was one of the guidelines for the medical system. The most prominent achievement of that time was anesthesia by acupuncture. The Frontline news frequently reported some successful cases. In addition to curing the dumb and deaf children, the most amazing cases were that the surgeons could perform operations on patients with the anesthesia by acupuncture. According to newspapers, the surgeons could talk to patients whose chests or bellies were opened for operations. In some cases, the operations were performed in some special operation rooms where there was a glass dome in the ceiling. It was also reported that surgeons, all over the world, came to watch such miraculous operations through the glass dome.

After we finished harvesting and threshing the rice, it was already the winter of 1968. Major general *Hao*, the commander of the division under which our army farm belonged to, came to inspect our farm. He talked to the PLA officers as well as some graduates. Before leaving, he instructed the PLA officers to ensure that when we leave this farm, we would be not only ideologically good, but also physically stronger so that we can serve the country better.

After his inspection, he sent a medical group to our farm and did a physical checkup for all of us. I happened to suffering from coughing. A military doctor gave me some medicine and my coughing was gone in a couple of days.

Based on General *Hao*'s instructions, our company established a fishing group. About 10 graduates were selected. This group's sole task was to catch fish. From then on, we had seafood in our meals.

There was not much to work on in the field during the cold winter. The PLA leaders arranged full-day political study. A main project for the political study was so-called "Political Camping." This involved marching to the nearby people's communes, carrying our bedrolls like soldiers. We were to live in the peasants' families of the Poor and Lower-Middle classes, to eat meals at their houses, and to chat with them. At the same time, we would also help them with some household chores. According to Chairman Mao: "The cleanest are workers and peasants, although their hands are dark, their feet were covered with cattle shit, they are still cleaner than the bourgeoisie and petty bourgeoisie intellectuals." We were to be re-educated by those peasants.

One day, we had a "Recalling Bitterness" educational session. This was a typical form of political education originated from the PLA. Such sessions were frequently held during the civil war. The soldiers from poor peasant families were encouraged to tell their sad family stories and attributed them to the KMT rule. Should the communist lost to the KMT, the sad time would return. This was quite successful to mobilize soldiers to fight in the civil war.

After the PRC was founded, this approach was gradually introduced to civilian people in order to let people appreciate the glory of this new socialist society and be thankful to the Party.

The speaker was the oldest poor peasant in the production team (a unit inside a people's commune, and is basically a village), and was expected to tell us the great bitterness under the KMT rule. Like many such poor peasants lived in the old China, he was illiterate. Walking slowly to the small podium and sitting down, he started. Because he was told that he was to give a speech to a group of college graduates, he started:

"I have 5000 *Yuan* in the bank (as a comparison, a college graduate's starting salary was 43.5 *Yuan* a month at that time), you may not have such a sum. But what was good about this? I am illiterate. You have finished college education, so you will be the beam and column of our country..."

The old man seemed to deviate from the required topic, so the production team leader interrupted him:

"Please tell them what bitterness you have experienced in your life."

"Oh, talking about the bitterness, the worst in my life was in 1960, we felt hungry all the time and there was no enough food."

Noticing some audience's funny expression, he sensed something might have gone wrong, so he quickly said:

"The party is great! Under President *Liu*'s '*San Zi Yi Bao*' (three Selves and one Contract policy), the situation quickly improved..."

I glanced at our political instructor, he lowered his head and could not refrain from laughing. This situation was like a comic performance, because at the earlier stage of the Cultural Revolution, President *Liu* was called "Khrushchev of China," and his "three Selves and one Contract" policy was among his biggest political mistakes. Especially, just a couple of weeks before, we studied a document issued by the Party's central committee, which denounced President *Liu* as "the big traitor, big spy, and big scab." *Liu* was deprived of all his posts inside and outside of the Party, and booted out of the Party "forever."[76] This old man apparently did not pay attention to the events in the Cultural Revolution, and did not understand the complexity of the situations. Moreover, he could not write a note for the leaders to preview, nor could he read a prepared script for his presentation. He just spoke offhand.

Fortunately, due to his red background and his grandfatherly senior age, he was well respected by the villagers, according to the old Chinese tradition. His misspoken comments did not bring him any trouble. In other cases, this could lead to some grave political consequences.

A commune officer also gave us a report about the Cultural Revolution in colleges. He had led a Mao Zedong propaganda team to work in the L-province University of Agriculture, where there was a professor specialized in grafting of plants. One of his research projects involved in grafting a purple eggplant with a light green eggplant. As a result, he was

---

[76]   *Liu* was rehabilitated in 1980 after the end of the Cultural Revolution.

able to produce a new eggplant with a light green background and purple spots on the skin.

"What difference does it make? After all, it was just an eggplant," he remarked.

"One day we pulled over a horse and asked this professor to look at the teeth and tell us how old the horse was." This officer continued:

"You know what? He told us he was not specialized in animals! Telling the age of a horse by looking at its teeth is something we peasant know very well. But a professor in the University of <u>Agriculture</u> does not know. He is the typical bourgeois professor! Our great leader Chairman Mao said: 'The lowly are more intelligent; the elite is more stupid.' We cannot let such bourgeois intellectuals to control our universities!"

Consequently, intellectuals obtained a new nickname: "Stinking ninth." It was well-know that there were eight black types: The Landlord and the Rich Peasant, the Capitalist, the counter-revolutionist, the bad elements, the Rightist, the traitor, the spy, and the Capitalist Roader. Now, "the Stinking Intellectual" was informally added to the Black Eight Types, ranked at the ninth place to become Number Nine, or "*Lao Jiu*" in Chinese.

In one of the Revolutionary Model Operas "Take Tiger Mountain by Strategy", a revolutionary hero entered into the bandit den and successfully posed himself as the Chair Number Nine. Then he passed the intelligence about the bandit's defense system, and helped his comrade to eradicate this bandit. Because the hero was called *Lao Jiu*, or Number Nine, this coincidence made all intellectuals somewhat liked this informal nickname, and frequently referred to themselves as "Number Nine" with this revolutionary hero in their minds.

In early March, battles between China and Soviet Union broke out on the *Zhenbao* Island. In our political study, we saw photos showing how the soviet officers and soldiers bullied Chinese citizens reported in the newspapers. Especially, the "Cripple Captain" was singled out as the bad guy. He was a first lieutenant and his leg was injured in some fighting with the Chinese. Because of the injury, he was rewarded and promoted to a captain. During the border conflict in March, he was killed by the PLA soldiers, together with most of his troops. A Soviet Tank was caught and later displayed in Beijing's Military Museum.

Spring came. Our water reservoir was filled with the water from the L-river and we were preparing to plant new crops.

In the evening on March 30, when we were doing a political study as usual, a fellow, who was responsible for inspecting irrigation system, ran in and said that the dam of the water reservoir had a crack and was leaking water. So, our platoon jumped up into action. Bring spades and straw bags, we ran to the site.

When we arrived, we saw a 4-5 feet wide gap on the dam. We started to fill the straw bags with the soil and threw them into the gap. But the bags were washed away almost immediately. Seeing this, a couple of people jumped into the gap and link their arms to reduce the water speed. This was quite effective. With reduced water speed, the straw bags were able to stay where they were put. At that time, the temperature was about 40 °F, the people in the water were certainly feeling cold. So those in the water started singing the song of Mao Quotation:

"Determined, not afraid of sacrifice, overcome all difficulties, and strive for victory."

One of the most popular Mao Quotation Songs during the Cultural Revolution.

The gap was finally filled and we returned to our barracks triumphantly. The farm leaders praised us for the heroic action and we were all rewarded as the Good Comrade collectively for this week.

In April, 1969, the Ninth National Congress of the CPC was held. This was an important milestone. By that time, new revolutionary committees were established in all provinces, municipalities, and autonomous regions in the mainland. Chairman Mao's words in this congress: "This is a congress of unity and a congress of victory" were quoted in all newspapers. Also, "*Lin Biao* would be Chairman Mao's successor" was written into the newly revised constitution of the CPC.

This event made us feel that the tumultuous years had finally ended, and life might start going normal. At that time, there was a document from the central government advising people to stop royal dancing and other similar activities related to the Cult of personality.

One day in the summer, a graduate from the Middle-South Institute of Mining and Metallurgy suffered appendicitis. He was sent to a hospital near our army farm. Three weeks later, he returned and told us about his adventure.

When he was in the hospital waiting for the operation, a surgeon came to see him and encouraged him to adopt the anesthesia by Ear Acupuncture, developed by this hospital. During that time, the research in the acupuncture was quite active. New methods and new successful cases were frequently reported in the newspaper.

The ear acupuncture is a branch of the general acupuncture with very small needles applied to two ears only. The theory is based on the shape of the ear, which is similar to a baby in the womb with the earlobe corresponding to the head. There are acupoints on the ear associated with the corresponding organs of the body.

Upon hearing this proposal, he hesitated. Then the surgeon said to him:

"As a young man, you should be brave and supportive of the emerging technology, advocated by Chairman Mao."

In such a situation, he had to accept the proposal, although reluctantly. After being put on the operating bed, a curtain dropped to his shoulder to block his view of his body. Then the anesthetist came to put some small needles into his two ears, and connected the needles to an instrument with electric wires. When the instrument was turned on, he felt some stimuli to his ears, which were tolerable. After a while a nurse came to clean the operation area. He told the surgeon that he felt the cool liquid applied to his belly and was concerned.

"Don't worry! The beauty of the anesthesia by acupuncture is that only the pain is suppressed, other senses remain normal," the surgeon assured him.

Finally, the operation started. When the knife cuts on his belly, he felt a sharp pain and told the surgeon about it. The surgeon ordered the anesthetist to increase the stimuli. He could feel the stronger electric pulses in the ears. In the meantime, a nurse asked him to read together the Chairman Mao's quotation again and again:

"Being determined, not afraid of sacrifice, overcome all difficulties, and achieve the victory."

The pain appeared subdued, and the surgeon continued to cut deeper. But once the surgeon started pulling his intestine to look for the appendix, he felt a strong and unbearable urge to vomit. He cried loudly. Immediately a mask was put onto his face and he quickly lost consciousness.

When he woke up, the operation was over and he was lying on a bed in a ward.

"I still feel sick when recalling that terrible moment," he told us.

July 18, 1969, we woke up from the noon nap by a sudden strong shake. Some people with earthquake experience shouted: "Earthquake! Run out!" We jumped out of the *Kang* and ran out. But there was no damage to our houses.

After dinner, we were notified that a 7.4 earthquake occurred at 1:25 p.m. in *Bohai* Sea. There was a possibility that a tsunami, or *Hai Xiao* in Chinese, might come to the coast where our army farm was located.

There was a dike to prevent the tide from entering the rice field. The leaders of the army farm decided that we were to protect the dike against the tsunami. About 20 minutes later, all of us arrived at the dike with shovels and straw bags. Each company was assigned a section of the dike to protect. For the time being we were sitting cross-legged on the ground, because we did not know whether the tsunami would come to us.

Without modern communication tools, we had to use some primitive method to determine the direction of the tsunami. A couple of people were ordered to measure the sea level every 10 minutes. If the water level went up quickly, it would indicate that the tsunami was coming this way, so we would start filling the straw bags and add them to the dike.

We were quietly sitting there watching the twinkling stars. Nobody said anything. Most of us lived inland since we were born and knew very little about the tsunami. We knew these words because it was in one of Chinese idiom *Shan Hu Hai Xiao*, which literally means mountain is yelling and sea is roaring. This idiom does not give any scientific clue about the natural phenomenon tsunami. With good swimming skills, I was quite relaxed. Then a fellow sitting next to me quietly elbowed me, and handed me a cigarette.

"You know I do not smoke," I replied with a smile.

"Come on! Smoke one," he begged.

I took his offer and felt something unusual. This made me uneasy. But again, my swimming skills reassured me.

The observers reported the water levels several times. It seemed that the water level kept going down. Around midnight, our leaders received a military radio call saying that the tsunami had moved in the opposite direction to *Tianjin*, so we went back to our barracks.

The second day, when eating breakfast, the fellow who handed me the cigarette, and was from local areas, told me the story about a tsunami happened in this area about 100 years ago. The water was like a high wall quickly moving ashore. Anything on its way was crushed, and the water even reached T-town, about 10 miles inland. So, we were lucky that the tsunami did not come in our direction.

It was not that the leaders of the army farm intentionally sent us to die, actually all the PLA leaders were with us. At that time, people generally had no idea about the tsunami, not even the college educated, such as us. Nor did we hear any news reports about the tsunamis from the radio stations or newspapers. The tsunami was so rare in China that this natural phenomenon was not taught in the classroom. On the other hand, through the propaganda everybody was educated that protecting state assets and properties was of the ultimate importance. For example, *Jin Xunhua*, a twenty-year-old Shanghai Educated Youth who sacrificed his life to save two wood electrical pools during a flood, was hailed as a hero and admitted posthumously as a member of the Communist Party. A large number of songs and poems were published to praise his heroics, and a postal stamp was also issued to commemorate him. In such an atmosphere, it would be natural to assume that it was worth any price to protect state assets and properties.

A couple of weeks later, we heard that many graduates in an army farm in *Guangdong* province went missing after their area had been struck by a typhoon. Two months later, we listened to a recording which was a speech given by a young man who managed to cling to life after being wiped into the ocean by this typhoon. He stayed afloat by holding a piece of wood, and was finally rescued by one of the PLA helicopters searching for survivors. He said that it was Mao Zedong thought that helped him to go through the ordeal:

"Each morning when I saw the sun rise, I would sing the song 'East is Red' which gave me enormous strength to hold on."

When he was lifted to the helicopter, the first words he uttered were "long live Chairman Mao!"

October 1, the National Day of the PRC, a dozen of graduates from our company went to YK-city for the holiday. In the downtown, we noticed a department store where many items were put near the main entrance and some crowd were gathered. We went there in the hope that there might be some good deals. Sure enough, a dozen or so violins were selling for 13 *Yuan*. The regular price for the entry level student violin was at least 60 *Yuan*. A decade ago, I had attempted to build a paper violin and failed.

Upon seeing these very affordable violins, I eagerly started selecting and bought one. Seeing I picked up one so quickly, several of my comrades thought it must be a good deal, and also picked up theirs. When we walked back, some people in the street thought we were from some Mao Zedong Thought Propaganda Team. They asked us where we would perform and wanted to follow us to watch—such a performance was free. We told them that we were not from any propaganda team, we bought that just to learn how to play the violin. The small crowd lost interest and went away.

We returned with our newly acquired toys and started playing. Some graduates from Beijing brought violins with them. They have some books about violin playing and etudes, such as a Chinese translation of "The Art of Violin Playing" by Carl Flesch, from which I took comprehensive notes. I also copied some etudes, such as "Wohlfahrt Sixty Studies." Both books were not available in the book stores since the Cultural Revolution started.

A few days after the National Day, I received a letter from my sister. She told me that our home was burned down due to a fire accident. Since returning in 1959, Mama had been living in the 16 Dragon lane, which was a two-story brick building, and was located in a good neighborhood.

Based on the class struggle situation, the Residential Committee[77] thought it was politically incorrect for a wife of a class enemy to continue living in such a good place. So, she was forced to move to a shanty area where houses were old and were built of wood plates.

Her new home was next to a small casting plant. In a dry and hot fall day, sparks started the fire. Since the lane was too narrow for a fire engine to drive in, when the firefighter finally put out the fire, the house was burned to the ground, my only photo album, all my books, and other belongings, which I did not bring with me to the Army Farm, were turned into ashes.

Learning my family tragedy, the PLA leaders of my company called me to the office. They expressed compassion to this unfortunate incident, and said that since there was no financial relationship between the PLA and my civilian unit, they could not provide me with any financial help. However, they decided to transfer me to the farm's repairing plant to do some work which was more industrial related. I understood that this was a way that they wanted to lift my spirit. I really appreciated their kindness.

In the last months of 1969, more and more *Xiao Dao Xiao Xi* (news through the grapevine) saying that we would leave the military farm in the near future, and work as engineers. It was in this atmosphere that we greeted the Chinese New Year in 1970.

Following the tradition, we had a big dinner with beer, wine, and *baijiu*, a strong Chinese liquor. We first finished all bottles of beers, then all bottles of red wines. Finally, only some bottles of liquor left. A couple of comrades proposed that we drink up all the remaining liquor. For the last group who still had the appetite to eat and drink, each one got a full bowel of 120 proof *baijiu*. We seeped the liquor slowly, talked excitingly about our future, our plans, and our new life as engineers, until it was past midnight.

Our PLA leaders also came to cheer up with us. Realizing that this might be the last Chinese New Year we spent together, both the PLA leaders and we expressed good wishes to each other.

---

[77] The Residential Committee was the lowest level of the citizen management system in China. It managed a certain number of residential families in coordination with the corresponding the public security station.

March 20, 1970, we left the military farm. We were to report to different provincial bureaus of metallurgy to be assigned new jobs.

I was to report to the J-province bureau of metallurgy in N-city. On the way back to N-city, I stayed in Beijing for a couple of days to see my uncle and younger brother. By then, my uncle had been released from the "cowshed" and had started working in the boiler room, shoveling coal into a boiler, instead of researching on making alloys. Since he was one of a couple of top alloy experts, I commented that it was a waste of talent for him to do such physical labor. But he appeared content, and said that this physical activity was good for his health, and that now he could sleep well, and had a good appetite.

My younger brother married in 1969, after they completed their training and assigned to teach at the same school. He was teaching mathematics, his wife was teaching Chinese literature.

He told me that a dozen political criminals had been executed shortly before I arrived. There was a mass rally in the Worker's Stadium in Beijing for an open trial. One of the condemned was 27 years old young man, named *Yu Luke,* who wrote a well-known article during the Cultural Revolution: "On Family Background," which criticized the class line policy. He argued that it was unfair to use the family background as a major factor to determine someone's future. This article was widely circulated and I also read it. Mr. *Qi Benyu,*[78] a member of powerful CCRG, declared that this article was a big poisonous weed. So, *Yu Luoke*'s fate was doomed. [79]

---

[78] Mr. *Qi Benyu* was jailed in the middle of the Cultural Revolution and sentenced to 18 years in prison in 1980.

[79] Mr. *Yu Luoke* was rehabilitated in 1979, after the end of the Cultural Revolution.

F-city (1970-1972)

After reporting to the J-province Bureau of Metallurgy, I was assigned to work in a newly established steel works in F-city. In the middle of April, I reported to F-city Steel Works. The five classmates who went to the army farm were all assigned jobs here.

The Steel Works was still in its early stage of construction. Following the supreme directive "Industry learns from *Daqing*", one of the famous oil corporation in China, which had a slogan: "Put production first and living secondary," there was no living facility in the factory when we arrived. Only the first blast furnace and its associated facilities were under construction. We temporarily lived in the guest house of the city government. Five of us were all assigned to the equipment department, and the tasks were checking the warehouse of the railroad station to see what equipment had arrived, and what had not. Then we'd arrange trucks to carry the arrived equipment to the production area for installation, and call the suppliers, asking them to send the not-yet-shipped equipment as soon as possible.

The production area was in the suburb of the city, and took about 30 minutes walking from the guest house. In the production area, there is a small hill which looked like a huge turtle. On the top of the hill, a reservoir was built to store water. The height of the hill could generate required water pressure. At the foot of the hill, there was an artificial lake formed by a dam. The water in the lake was pumped into the reservoir as the source of the cooling water.

It was quite popular during that time that some special dates were natural deadlines for construction projects. May Day was the deadline for producing the first batch of cast iron, as the gift to Chairman Mao and the Party. One day, there was a test run for the cooling water system. When the main valve was turned on, the high-pressure water cracked one pipe, and the water was like a fountain, spraying to the sky. The valve had to be shut off. When the party secretary of the Steel Works heard the news, he immediately asked who the designer of that system was.

"Arrest that engineer!" He yelled.

But the design was done by the N-city Design Institute of Metallurgy, which was not under his leadership. After learning this news, the head of the design institute asked to check the design. There was nothing wrong. Instead, the failure was due to the quality of the cast iron pipe. The design specifications required that the pipe would be produced by Shanghai Factory of Cast Iron Pipes. However, to buy industry equipment outside the province must be approved by the top leader of the province. Our supply manager had to see General *Sheng*, now the Party Secretary of J-province Revolutionary Committee, for permission.

"Why must you buy the pipes from Shanghai? Don't we have a factory that can produce cast iron pipes?" Asked general *Sheng*.

"Yes, we do. But our cast iron pipes were for drainage which handles low pressure water. The pipe produced by Shanghai Factory was for high pressure water." The supply manager explained.

"Nonsense! I do not believe Shanghai's moon is rounder than ours!" Mr. *Sheng* declared:

"Equipped with the invincible Mao Zedong thought, we can create any miracle!"

The supply manager dared not to argue with this flamboyant leader. As a result, the pipe produced by local factory was used, and then burst under the high pressure of the cooling water.

Now it was clear that this incident was not the fault of the design engineer. On the other hand, workers in local factory were proletarian, the leading class of this country. They were beyond blaming. General *Sheng* finally approved the purchase from the Shanghai factory. The new pipes were quickly transported and installed by the fitters working around the clock. By May Day, the blast furnace produced the first batch of cast iron. We successfully turned in our May Day gift to Chairman Mao and the Party.

After a month or so in the equipment department, I was tired of the management oriented work. Since the blast furnace had started running, I wanted to go there to gain more technical experience. After applying for it, I was transferred to the blast furnace plant. This afforded me the opportunity to refresh the knowledge of iron production I learned in the college.

One day, General *Sheng* came to inspect our factory. After reviewing the production, he gave us a speech.

"Look! Isn't the blast furnace like a spoiled bourgeois boy?" *Sheng* asked. Noticing his audience was puzzled, he explained:

"Each blast furnace has three hot blast stoves to serve it. At the same time, it also needs water to cool its steel shell. So, it cannot bear cold, nor heat. These are typical shortcomings of the bourgeois. So, we should have a revolt against it!"

"Why can't we just dig the hill to make a blast furnace?" *Sheng* continued.

At that moment, one engineer stood up and said:

"Commissar *Sheng*'s[80] idea is really inspiring! I figured out a way to implement this revolutionary idea."

General *Sheng* smiled at that engineer and said:

"Very good! Come and explain it."

The engineer walked to the podium and started to explain:

"First, we dig a hole based on certain sized blast furnace, then add a layer of chamotte brick as we do for the normal blast furnace. Then we put a coiled steel pipe at the top. The cold air can go through the coiled pipe and would be heated by the heat generated during the iron making process. This would eliminate the hot blast stoves. Such a blast furnace without the steel shell would not need a water-cooling system because the hill would not melt."

Without calculation of the detailed heat exchange, the idea appeared plausible, and appreciated by General *Sheng*. He praised:

"See! As long as an intellectual is equipped with the invincible Mao Zedong thought, he could create things that capitalist engineers cannot think of!"

---

[80] During the Cultural Revolution, many PLA officers went to work in civilian organizations. Calling them by their military ranks was the preferred way of addressing these leaders, because civilian titles, such as secretary, had been associated with the Capitalist Roader.

After three months, an experimental "hill blast furnace" was finished, and a test run was scheduled. We went to the Fire-Starting ceremony. After that, the head of the plant ordered: "Start!" Raw materials were put into the furnace from the top, based on the proper ratio, and then the fire started.

Eight hours later, it was time to get the liquid iron out of the furnace. We went to see it again. After the taphole was opened, nothing flowed out. The workers looked into the hole and saw that the charcoal was burned out, but the limestone and iron ore were still in their solid shapes. After a long silence, the head of the plant used a long coop to take one piece of the limestone.

"If that furnace cannot make iron, but can make lime, then our efforts would not be totally wasted." He said.

But after breaking the pieces of limestone, he saw only the thin outside layer that had become lime, and the inside was still hard limestone, so he threw up both hands, and then walked away without a single word.

One day in August when I was eating dinner in the dining hall, a middle-aged man came and shared the small dining table with me. As usual, he started a small chat. He introduced himself as *Lao Zhao* (Old *Zhao*, this is the most common way to call other older people, or when a man introduces himself to younger people), and said he was the head of this company's design group. Then he asked me about my working unit, and my educational background, etc. When he heard that I had majored in metallurgical machinery, and was a graduate of the 1967 school year, he was interested. By May of 1966 when the Cultural Revolution started, we already had finished four years of course work, and we're doing graduation practice. He thought I was qualified as a real college graduate.

"When I attended the college before the Liberation, everyone studied only four years. This five-year system was copied from the Soviet Union by adding a graduation project," he said.

He told me that his group needed more hands doing the design work, and asked me if I was interested in joining his team.

"Absolutely!" I answered without hesitation because this was my dream work. I had studied very hard to prepare myself for this job. He wrote down my name and working unit with a big smile. A few days later, the head of our department called me to his office, and announced the transfer. I was elated.

After reporting to work, I was given a desk with a drawing board, and necessary instruments. A senior engineer Ms. *Yu* was assigned as my supervisor. She gave me a small design task. When I submitted my drawing for her to review, I could tell from her smiling face that she was happy. After finishing my small design project, I was assigned to work with a team of engineers from the N-city Design Institute of Metallurgy. The engineers were specialized in various areas. I was the only employee from the F-city Steel Works. We were to work on a big project of designing a pipe rolling plant. Since there was no enough space in the guest house of F-city, I went to N-city to work with those engineers on their campus.

At that time, Mama was living in N-city, and I was able to live with her and commute to work. Upon arriving, Mama handed me a blueprint of a piston ring which was used in a walking tractor. General *Sheng* had launched a mass campaign to produce walking tractors by all the residents in the city. He asked each family to produce one part of a walking tractor so that a certain number of tractors could be built for the agricultural mechanization. For a small family like my mother herself, one piston ring was her task. On the blueprint, the piston ring looks simple to a novice, just a circle with a notch. But its manufacturing requires high precision machining tools.

"What equipment does your Residential Committee have?" I asked.

"Nothing, not even a file! We were supposed to resolve all the related problems by ourselves," Mother told me.

How could people make a piston ring bare-handedly? This made me recall the mass campaign of iron and steel making in 1958. A couple of months later, this campaign was quietly called off, perhaps because General *Sheng* finally realized the absurdity of his fantasy.

Our design project started with visiting corporations that had similar machines as that we planned to build. The engineers in the design institution selected a couple of steel factories to visit. We were to listen to the machine operators' opinions about the pros and cons of the existing machines. Then, in our design, we were to combine as many pros as possible and figure out ways to overcome the shortcomings.

On our way back, I stopped at S-city train station to see my maternal grandmother, who had been living with the family of my fourth aunt since he left Beijing in 1966. She suffered a stroke in 1969. As a result, her right half was paralyzed, and could not speak. She was happy to see me, and smiled brightly. She held my arm with her left hand and looked at me carefully, and uttered some sounds that I could not understand. Then she gestured to let me talk to my aunt, uncle, and cousins. This was the last time I saw her. She passed away one year later at the age of 89.

One weekend, when walking in the street, I ran into my high school classmate Mr. *Su*, who was the secretary of the Youth League of our class, and was admitted to the Department of Automatic Control at Tsinghua University. I noticed another classmate Ms. *Xiong, who* was next to him, and was apparently pregnant.

After a chat, I learned that Mr. *Su* was assigned to work in a factory in *Harbin* after his graduation. Ms. *Xiong* studied veterinary and was assigned to work on a farm near N-city. After their marriage, Mr. *Su* managed to transfer from *Harbin* to the farm town. He said that he did not accustom to the cold weather in *Harbin*. After joining his wife, he worked on that farm as an electrician to maintain and repair simple farming equipment. Learning that I was doing mechanical design, he showed an air of admiration, and said:

"You are really lucky to be able to do the job you are trained for."

I felt sorry for Mr. *Su*. If his knowledge in automatic control was not used soon, it would go rusty.

In a couple of months, our tasks were finished. Then I returned to F-city, and was waiting for the order to start the manufacturing process. At that time, our company did not have the capability to manufacture most of the machine parts because of inadequate machine tools. We needed other factories to help with the manufacturing and installation.

While I was not there, a couple of hundred workers were recruited from the countryside. Some houses with rammed earth walls were built to accommodate them. This was to follow the Supreme Directive of Chairman Mao:

"In industry, learn from *Daqing*."

The wall built with rammed earth was very common in the north and west of China because these areas have more snows than rains. *Daqing* is in the North-East of China. This was why the rammed earth wall had been used there. But in southern China, there are more rains and less snow. The rammed earth wall would crack in the southern moist climate. Upon seeing the cracks on the walls, bamboo sheds were built quickly to transfer the workers to the sheds. The rammed earth houses were abandoned. I found a room in the shed and lived there.

A few days later, I was transferred to a newly established electro-mechanic group. Mr. *Liu*, the head of this group, was recently transferred here from a mining company. The tasks of this group were to provide equipment for the factory. If the equipment could be bought ready-made, then we would buy it. Otherwise, we'd design and manufacture it. Mr. *Liu* managed to transfer my other four classmates to his group. We worked together again.

In late spring, one of the leaders in the factory returned from an organized visit to *Jinggang* Mountain, the famous revolutionary base established by Chairman Mao in 1927. The leader gave us a report about the newly remodeled *Jinggang* Mountain Revolutionary Museum. He showed a photo of the oil painting: "Join Force in *Jinggang*." This was a famous painting that had been published in newspapers and magazines. Making a comparison between this photo and the one I saw before, I found Marshall *Zhu De* was changed to *Lin Biao*. Moreover, in the elementary school our textbook had a lesson "*Zhu De's* carrying-pole," which tells the story about the carrying-pole with *Zhu De's* name. Since there were no enough carrying-poles for everybody on *Jinggang* red base, and Marshall *Zhu* wanted to take part in the laboring activities, he wrote his name on one of the carrying-poles: "*Zhu De De Bian Dian* (*Zhu De's* carrying-pole)." This way, he would be able to labor together with his soldiers every time.

However, after this remodeling, *Zhu De's* carrying-pole was removed. Instead, the carrying-pole with *Lin Biao's* name was on display. It was said that some concerned workers mentioned that in real history, it was *Zhu De's* carrying-pole. General *Sheng* replied:

"History should serve the Revolution!"

It is likely that this leader also learned in his school about *"Zhu De's carrying-pole,"* when he said:

"During the visit," he hesitated a little and then said quickly with lowered voice: "We also saw vice chairman *Lin Biao's* Carrying Pole."

In July 1971, an explosive news was announced that Mr. Henry Kissinger had visited China, and President Richard Nixon would visit China in the future. Only one year before, on May 20 1970, did Chairman Mao publish a declaration: "People of the world Unite to Defeat the American Aggressor and All of its Running Dogs." This was known as 5-20 Declaration. The official newspapers did not elaborate about Mr. Kissinger's visit. The short news only mentioned that he had visited China and made the arrangement for President Nixon's to visit China in February of 1972.

In China, there is a newspaper called "Reference News," which publishes the selected translation of the articles from foreign media. At that time, "Reference News" could only be subscribed by the cadre ranked eighteen-grade or higher. Mr. *Liu*, our unit leader, subscribed it, so we could borrow it from him. In "Reference News" there were more details about Kissinger's visit and his meetings with Premier *Zhou Enlai*. Actually, there were a prelude before this drama, known as Ping Pong diplomacy.

Upon hearing this news, we were all excited about this historic breakthrough between the two great countries. All my friends and acquaintances reacted positively to this news. As a Chinese saying goes: one would not fear to have a lot of friends, but would fear to have a single enemy. Reducing an enemy would be warmly welcomed by the general public, especially in the situation that Albania, "the bright light along the coast of the Adriatic Sea," as praised by the official media, was the only Marxist friend of China.

Soon after the Chinese New Year in 1972, President Nixon visited China and signed the well-known Shanghai Communique. The historical picture of Chairman Mao shook hands with President Nixon appeared on the front pages of all newspapers.[81] Many of my friends and I believe this historical handshaking opened a new era of international relationship.

---

[81] This made President Nixon one of the most famous, as well as most popular American presidents in China. When he resigned, many Chinese genuinely felt sorry for him.

It is well-known that after the Liberation, the United States immediately became an archenemy because it was regarded as the number one imperialist country and also because it supported the KMT government during the Chinese Civil war. Since then, even listening to "Voice of America" was a counter-revolutionary crime, and could be jailed. In early 1950s, merely saying "America" could cause trouble. The politically correct way of referring to the United States was "the paper tiger." The Korean war further damaged the relationship between the two countries. After breaking up with Khrushchev, the enemies of China were classified in three groups: the imperialist countries headed by the United States, the revisionist countries, mainly the east European countries, headed by the Soviet Union, and counter-revolutionary forces represented by Chiang Kai-shek's government.

Now the "paper tiger" suddenly became a friend, or non-enemy to say the least, we all welcomed this new development and the added power against the "Soviet New Czar." This historical event was hailed in newspapers as a great strategic move by our visionary helmsman, Chairman Mao.

Soon after the electro-mechanic group was established, a new project was assigned to us. We were to provide the equipment for the BOF steel making plant. Based on the workflow, this plant should be built before the pipe rolling plant. I was responsible for the oxygen blown mechanism for the converter. The BOF practicing experience in Shanghai in 1966 was of great help. By October 1 1971, the National Day, I finished my design work. Next step was to arrange the manufacturing. I got permission from the provincial leaders to arrange the manufacturing in J-steel Corp. Since then, I frequently had business trips to this steel corporation.

Near the end of September in 1971, we received a notice from the central government that there would be no National Day Parade. The notice explained that this was to let people have a good rest.

After the National Day, I went to nearby J-steel Corp to check the progress of the manufacturing process. At the guest house, I met several people from other parts of the country. They started telling the news about a plane crash. Nobody dared to give details. When we pieced together the information through the grapevine, it was clear that something went wrong with *Lin Biao*, Chairman Mao's closest comrade-in-arms and the "heir apparent." *Lin Biao* did not show up when Chairman Mao met with Ethiopia's emperor Haile Selassie in Early October. Before this, Mao and *Lin* had been always appearing together since 1966. Moreover, his name no longer appeared in the newspaper.

Finally, in November, a document from the CPC Central Committee was announced to us in the all-hands meeting of our Steel Works, and officially accused *Lin Biao* as the traitor, who attempted to flee to the revisionist Soviet Union. His plane crashed in Mongolia on September 13, 1971. Actually, by November, most people had already learned the news through the grapevine, and were not shocked by this announcement.

Among the materials distributed for denouncing *Lin Biao*, the most intriguing document was "Project 571."

The number 571 and the phrase "armed uprising" were somewhat homophonous in Chinese. In this document, Chairman Mao was given the code name "B-52," and referred to as *dang dai qin shi huang* (current "first emperor of *Qin* Dynasty"). Additional documents also revealed the alleged plans to assassinate Chairman Mao when he was travelling and inspecting some southern provinces. But Chairman Mao was very alert and randomly changed his travelling schedule. So, the assassination attempts failed.

The episodes described in those documents were like intrigues in royal courts described in many classical novels. We were utterly baffled to see that *Lin Biao*, who had initiated the movement to study Chairman Mao's books, praised Chairman Mao as the genius that could only appear every few hundred years, and his would-be-heir was written into the Constitution of the Party, would develop such plans.

My project went into high gear near the end of 1971. I frequently went to J-steel Corp to inspect the machine parts manufactured there. One evening after dinner some fellow travelers in the guest house and I went to watch an open-air movie. On the way, we saw there was a gathering in an open area. Out of curiosity we went to see what was going on. Walking near, we saw a lady in her late 30s standing in the middle of the crowd with a placard hanging on her neck. The characters on the placard were "Worn out Shoe XXX". "Worn out shoe" is an old Chinese nickname for women who have extramarital affairs.

A man called the start of the meeting and asked the lady:

"You are married. Why do you behave like this?"

"My husband is in Shanghai, not here." The lady answered simply.

"Doesn't the government give you the Home Leave[82] every year?" The man asked.

"The Home Leave is of 12 days only. But the love-making is something like meal, we need it every day!"

Her words were followed by a thunderous laughter. I called my fellows to go, or the best spots would be occupied. So, we hurried off to the open-air movie site. It was one of the model Beijing operas: "The Legend of the Red Lantern." During the first 7-8 years of the Cultural Revolution, the eight so-called Model Plays[83] were all we could entertain.

As before, making the first batch of steel was the planned New Year's gift for Chairman Mao and the Party. In the New Year's Eve of 1972, we managed to produce the first batch of steel with our converter. The propaganda department came to take pictures, as usual, for writing reports to the upper level leaders.

However, the supporting equipment was not yet ready. I was given a new task to design a gantry crane to unload the steel making materials from the cargo train. I worked so hard on the drawing board that I got frostbites on both my hands.

As usual, after the New Year's Day, we entered the holiday season because the Chinese New Year, or the Spring Festival, would soon follow. Most people take the Home Leave during that time. By combining the twelve-day Home Leave with the Chinese New Year holidays, they can stay with their families longer.

Mr. *Li*, an old electrician in our working unit, stayed, because he had already used up his Home Leave to attend his son's wedding ceremony in October of 1971. There were some other co-workers in our unit also stayed, including me because I was busy working on the design task. Mr.

---

[82] In Mao's era, all city workers were given 12 days paid Home Leave. For the married couple, this vacation was used to see the spouse. For the unmarried, this vacation was used to visit their parents if they lived in different places.

[83] The eight model plays consist of five Beijing operas, two ballets and one symphony,

Li cordially invited us to his small house for the traditional dinner in the Chinese New Year's Eve. After downing a couple of 120 proof liquor, Mr. *Li* became talkative and started talking about himself. He was born in a village in JS-province, and went to Shanghai to search for prosperity. Starting as an apprentice and working hard for three years, he graduated and became an electrician.

He told us:

> "Each Chinese New Year's eve, the shop owner would give us double wage for the month. But since 1958, I have not gotten a single penny raise by our people's government."[84]
> He complained.

We all knew that since 1958, the government had not given anybody a raise. But only the member of the Proletarian Class, like Mr. *Li* dared to complain openly.

He continued talking about another subject, saying:

> "I did not like gambling, nor did I like Opium. But I did like going to brothels. In Shanghai, there were different brothels. The higher priced ones were like luxury hotels with restaurants. The prostitute would accompany the client all the time. In the cheapest ones, you get in from the front door, pay the money, do your business, and get out from the back door. My money was all gone that way. But you know what? It turned out to be good."

He paused to sip the liquor, then continued:

"Otherwise, my wife would ask me to buy land, as did one of my fellow countrymen, who lived frugally in Shanghai, and saved money to buy land in the home village, especially just before the Liberation when the land was cheap. Alas! During the early 1950s land reform, he was denounced and then executed as the Landlord, and his land confiscated and redistributed. Had I followed the suit, I would not be here tonight!"

---

[84] At that time, nearly all city workers were government employees and paid by the central government.

We all laughed.

After I finished the design, a different company called Sixth Corp was to build the gantry crane. It took them a month or so to finish the job and erected the steel structure in the field where the steel making materials were to be stored. The next step was to add the driving system that would move the crane on its rails.

Then the news came that this Steel Works was part of *Lin Biao*'s secret plot to establish his own base. And General *Sheng* was arrested and jailed.[85] So all constructions were ordered to stop. For months, the whole company was in disarray. People went to work around 8:00 a.m. as usual. But by 9:00 a.m., they were all back to the dormitory because there was nothing to do.

In the meantime, another political campaign started: reading the classic books of Marxism-Leninism. *Lin Biao* was perhaps the most eminent advocate to promote Chairman Mao's books. It was the PLA that first compiled and published the Chairman Mao's quotation, known as "the little red book." He wrote a well-known inscription: "Read Chairman Mao's books; listen to Chairman Mao's words; act according to Chairman Mao's directives; be Chairman Mao's good soldiers." These words were printed on the first page of the "little red book."

Shortly after the downfall of *Lin Biao*, one of Chairman Mao's letters written to his wife *Jiang Qing* in 1966, was published as an official document. According to the letter, Chairman Mao criticized *Lin Biao* about promoting his works: "Some of his saying made me uneasy. I never believed that my lowly books could have such a magic effect."

As a result, Chairman Mao advised people to study original books written by Marx, Engels, Lenin, and Stalin. Among the books he recommended were Chinese translations of "Communist Manifesto" by Marx and Engels, "A Contribution to the Critique of Political Economy" by Karl Marx, "Anti-Dühring," "Dialectics of Nature," "Ludwig Feuerbach and the End of German Classical Philosophy" by Engels, and "The State and Revolution" by Lenin. All employees with a college education were given the set of the translated books to study. I felt that those books were

---

[85]   General *Sheng* was detained from 1972 to 1978, jailed from 1978 to 1982, and passed away in 2004.

not only irrelevant to my daily work as a mechanical engineer, but also were obscure to read. I never finished any of the books. I noticed that during the discussion sessions, nobody was able to speak anything in depth. We just quoted the words in articles published in the newspapers and magazines to pretend that we had read and understood those topics, and could say something about them.

During that time, one extramarital affair occurred between our dispatcher Mr. *Lei* and a lady Ms. *Cha,* who worked in our drafting department, tracing drawings. Both were married. Mr. *Lei* was in his middle 30s and his wife worked in Shanghai, while Ms. *Cha* was in her late 20s and her husband worked in N - city. First, Ms. *Cha* and Mr. *Lei* exchanged some love notes. Although Ms. *Cha* asked Mr. *Lei* to destroy those notes after reading, Mr. *Lei* kept one he treasured the most. He even brought the note to Shanghai when he took his Home Leave. As a result, this note was discovered by his wife. Infuriated, his wife wrote a letter to the head of our Steel Works with Ms. *Cha's* love note attached.

A series of meetings was held in our organization to criticize the two. In one of the meetings, Mr. *Lei* confessed how this affair started. One evening, he went to the city guest house to watch an open-air movie. Ms. *Cha* happened to be there also. After the movie, Ms. *Cha* invited Mr. *Lei* to her house in the city. Her son was with her husband in N-city under the care of her mother-in-law, so she was alone. At first, they sat outside. After a while, Ms. *Cha* complained about the mosquitoes and proposed to sit inside. Mr. *Lei* agreed. Inside the house, Ms. *Cha* said it was too hot, and took off her skirt and shirt wearing only the shorts. She also encouraged Mr. *Lei* to take off his shirt and pants to cool himself. When they were in shorts, she started to flirt with him. Then all of sudden Ms. *Cha* hugged Mr. *Lei* and turned off the light...

Mr. *Lei* remarked emotionally:

"Comrades, think about it! In such a situation, even the cadre who participated the long march[86] would not be able to resist it!"

I looked around and noticed everyone trying to refrain from laughing. After the meetings, Ms. *Cha* was transferred to another company in N-city.

---

[86] The cadre who participated the famous long march was commonly regarded as the most iron-willed.

Mr. *Lei* was sent to the raw material department to do physical labor. It was perplexing that the physical labor was propagandized as the most glorious, and workers were proletarian class, i.e. the leading class. Yet, once an office worker, that is, a white collar worker, made mistakes, they would be sent to do physical labor as punishment.

Near our Steel Works, there was a Five-Seven Cadre School. Its name came from the Chairman's supreme directive on May 7, 1966, which called on the people to make the whole nation a big school, to learn their own profession, as well as other trades, like the PLA had done. Many capitalist roaders, cow demons, snake spirits, and the like were sent to such schools to learn "other trades." But it was actually a punishment, because those who were sent to Five-Seven Cadre School, were forced to do hard physical labor.

I noticed a bald-headed old gentleman grazing a water buffalo in the field. He often brought a big umbrella, opening it to create shade. He would lie under the shade to read books and let the buffalo graze by itself. One day, I tried to have a small talk with him. I first walked up and politely introduced myself. Hearing my self-introduction, he smiled amiably and asked me to sit down in the shade. From our talk, I learned that he was a vice minister at the Ministry of Light Industry, and had been denounced as a capitalist roader. He was locked up in a "cowshed" for a while, and then sent to this Five-Seven Cadre School to take care of this water buffalo. At first, he was afraid of this big animal with strong horns. But later he found this buffalo was quite tame. After a while, they established quite a good relationship, and the buffalo was able to understand his whistles and some simple word commands.

I noticed that he was reading the classical novel "Dreams in the Red Chamber," one of the classical novels praised by Chairman Mao, and was allowed to be reprinted during the Cultural Revolution.

Shortly after the October 1 National Day of 1972, I passed by him and saw him in a good mood, and smiling brightly. He told me that he had been "liberated" and would soon be back to his old post in Beijing. In those days, the word "liberation" meant rehabilitation and then a return to the original job position. I had a young colleague who was a son of the Minister of Electronic Industry. Also, during that time, he told me that his father had been liberated. He had been assigned a new job in Beijing to join his family. We held a small farewell party for him.

The news finally came in November that our Steel Works would be abandoned and all employees would be transferred to other companies. I learned that my alma mater needed five faculty members. I was very interested in teaching there, and went to see the officer who was responsible for the recruitment. Unfortunately, I was turned down because of my father's problem.

In December, I was transferred to the Factory of Heavy Machinery in X-city. About that time, my sister ended her reeducation in Sheng *Xin Farm*, and was assigned a job in YC-city as a lathe operator.

X-city (1972-1976)

A truck carried me and my stuff to X-city Factory of Heavy Machinery, which was established a couple of years ago. I was arranged to temporarily live in its guest house and share a room with another fellow employee, who also transferred from F-city Steel Works. Soon, Mr. *Wang*, the Party secretary of the factory, noticed me, because among my personal belongings was a violin. He had just set up a Mao Zedong Thought Propaganda Team, a small performing arts team. About a week later, I was in the band of the team. There were about 20 people altogether. After some preparation, we started performing in nearby people's communes and factories for the holiday seasons of the Chinese New Year.

After the holidays, we returned to our working units. I was assigned a task of designing a gantry saw to cut the log into planks, which were used for making wood molds for casting. The sawing was done by two workers push-pulling a huge log saw, and the productivity was very low.

As usual, I first went two factories in G-city where there were similar saws. I talked to the operators and made some notes.

Five years had passed since I left G-city in1968. Naturally, I found time to visit my Alma Mater. There was no big change except that the monument to the martyrs of the Cultural Revolution was gone. In 1970 when all students graduated and left, the central government issued a document, which ordered to demolish all the monuments for the people who died during the Cultural Revolution, because those monuments reflected the dark side of the Cultural Revolution, and would tarnish the image of the great, glorious, and the correct Communist Party.

Interestingly, I met the professor who taught us Russian and now was teaching English, after going to the language school to study English. This made me recall my high school Russian teacher who used to be an English teacher for years. After the Liberation, he was sent to language school to learn, and then to teach Russian.

One evening I went to the book store which was one of my favorite places to spend my spare time during my college years. Since the Cultural Revolution started, book stores carried only the political related books: Chairman Mao's selected works, and the works by Marx, Engels, Lenin, Stalin, etc., and also the booklets of the reprinted editorials of Red Flag, People's daily, and the PLA Daily. After 1969, some medical books for Bare-Foot-doctors were also published. I bought one such medical book whose preface reads like that of a political book, and was full of Chairman Mao's quotes and political jargons of the time.

While browsing the publications, I noticed a vinyl which was a pronunciation guide to International Phonetic Symbols. I gladly bought one, and planned to study English by myself. Publishing this vinyl could be a result of the President Nixon's visit. I also looked around to see if there were good textbooks, but unfortunately, I could find none. So, I went to a used book store nearby. Sure enough, I was able to find an old English textbook and one grammar book. Since I already had learned Russian, I thought I could apply my learning experience to guide my English study.

Returning to X-city, I reviewed my notes and evaluated the two machines. Then I formed my own design idea and finished the design. At that time, there was a common practice in the company that once a design task was assigned, the engineer was also responsible for organizing manufacturing and installation, until the machine was formally transferred to the plant that would use it.

During the installation stage, we hired some local peasants to help with the foundation work. Their task was to dig a rectangular hole so that concrete could be poured into it to form the foundation.

During breaks, I engaged in some small talks with them, and in China, such talks generally start with the families. I first talked to a peasant who looked older than others and appeared to be in his thirties. At such an age, most people in the countryside would have married and have some children. So, I naturally asked him how many kids he had. My question caused the other peasants to laugh. They told me that he did not even have a wife because he was a Landlord, and no girl would want to marry him. I was surprised because when the land reform occurred in the early 1950s, he might be around 10 years old. How could such a young kid be classified as a Landlord? As it turned out, it was his father who was classified as a Landlord. After his father died, the Landlord title was somewhat "inherited" by the son. Looking at the blushing "landlord Jr," I felt guilty for unwittingly having hurt him.

It was already late in April when the foundation was built. We were unlikely to be able to assemble the gantry saw, adjust it, and make it work. But we had promised to finish the gantry saw, and use it as the May Day gift to Chairman Mao and the Party. Our department leader found a quick solution: they hired a dozen peasants from a local commune to work on it. But they had never been trained in mechanical assembly and installation. What they did was to tighten the nuts after fitters put the right bolts into the holes. The peasants turned the nuts with all their maximum muscle strength, without any measurements of the alignments, the required clearances, and the allowed torques for some nuts. So, with this mass effort, the parts were indeed put together by April 30. But, when the electric switch was turned on, we heard only the electric motor humming, as the saw did not move.

Nevertheless, on May Day the propaganda department came to take pictures in front of the gantry saw, as planned, with smiling leaders shaking hands with us. The pictures would be included in the factory report to the superiors. The picture, after all, was a static image, it did not matter whether the machine was moving or not.

After this May Day ritual, a group of fitters came to rework the assembly and installation. Leading by an experienced head, the fitters brought various instruments, and assembled the parts slowly to make sure the technical requirements were met. When the installation was finished and the switch was turned on, the machine started to move as designed.

The master fitter looked new to me. He was indeed newly transferred from a factory in S-province. At the age of 42, he had worked as a fitter for decades. He was a good story teller. During the breaks, he told us a lot of interesting things about his old factory in S-province. Among his stories, the one about an old worker in his former factory impressed me the most.

One day, this worker saw that a Chairman Mao Badge had been

dropped into a small ditch, and was half covered with silt. Feeling that this sense did not look good, and that the silt was too dirty for him to pick it up by hand, he decided to push the badge all the way into the silt with a dried tree branch. As luck would have it, another worker was passing by while the old man was pushing the badge down. This worker reported to the factory leaders that this old man had blasphemed Chairman Mao by throwing the Mao badge into the open ditch and pushed it the dirty silt. That was a big political crime at that time, and a mass rally was convened. During the rally, the poor old man was denounced and declared as an active counter-revolutionist, even he defended himself with the above story. At the end of the rally, he was fired by the factory, and cuffed away by the local policemen.

In my design group, there was a middle-aged architect, Mr. *Chen*. We soon became good friends. His wife was a gynecologist working in the attached clinic. After the Liberation, women no longer changed their family names to the husbands' family names when they married. Like all other married women in China, Mrs. *Chen* was referred by her maiden family name as Dr. *Jiang*. Both of them were born in Hong Kong, and they were high school sweethearts.

In the early 1950s, responding to the call by the Party to build a new China, Mr. *Chen* went to *Guangzhou*, i.e. Canton city, to attend the H-N Institute of Engineering and majored in architecture. Two years later, Dr. *Jiang* followed suit to attend the H-N Institute of Medicine. After graduation in 1956, Mr. *Chen* was assigned a job in the Beijing Design Institute of Iron and Steel. Two years later, Dr. *Jiang* also graduated and was assigned a job in *Xiehe* Hospital (known as Peking Union Medical College Hospital in the West). They got married that year. In 1959, Beijing Mayor decided to "purify" Beijing politically by kicking out the problematic elements. Among them were those who had overseas relatives. At that time, Hong Kong was still a colony of England. So, Mr. *Chen* and Dr. *Jiang* were transferred from Beijing to N-city due to their oversea relationship. Mr. *Chen* worked in the Design Institute of Metallurgy, and Dr. *Jiang* worked at the Hospital for Women and Children.

Like most intellectuals in China, Mr. *Chen* was dedicated to his profession. As an architect, he bought a camera and took pictures of various buildings and structures when traveling, then put the pictures into his big notebooks. He neatly wrote his comments beside each picture, about the pros and cons of the building or structure from an architectural point of view.

When the Cultural Revolution started, his house was raided by Red Guards. These notebooks were confiscated and used as evidence of his bourgeois life style. Together with his many professional books, the notebooks were thrown into the fire. Seeing his treasured notebooks, which he spent a decade to accumulate, turned into ashes, his heart was broken. Similar to the 1959 "purifying Beijing," during the "cleaning class ranks" campaign in 1968, launched by General *Sheng*, Mr. *Chen*, Dr. *Jiang* and their young daughter and son were again kicked out of N-city, and sent to the countryside to be "re-educated" by the Poor and Lower-Middle peasants.

Since 1966, for five years, no single college had enrolled new students. When this factory was formed in 1970, there were no enough engineers. As a result, the *Chens* were liberated, and transferred from the village to this factory.

I had another colleague, *Wei Dong*, with some interesting story as well.

Since my college years I have developed a habit of morning jogging. Frequently when I started running, I could hear steps from the attached elementary school and saw a girl walking with a mop and a bucket. After a while, I discovered that she cleaned the school's public latrine every morning. There was no janitor hired for this job in this school. So, the school employees would take turn to clean it. She cleaned the latrine in the early morning so that other co-workers would not need to do this.

Later I learned that the girl was a high school student in her senior year and was ready to graduate when the Cultural Revolution started in 1966. During *Po Si Jiu* (Break Four Olds), *Li Si Xin* (Establish Four News) of the Cultural Revolution, there was a trend to rename the streets that were regarded as old fashioned, or not revolutionary. In the meantime, after the speech of *Tan Lifu*, mentioned earlier, it was in vogue for youngsters from the families of Black Types to publicly denounce their parents, to draw a clear line of demarcation from their families, and to change the names given by their "black" parents. This girl's parents owned a shop, and therefore were classified as the Capitalist, which was one of Black Types. She changed her given name to "*Wei Dong*," one of the popular names those days, and adopted by many youngsters. In Chinese *Wei* means defend or protect, *Dong* is the last Chinese character in Chairman Mao's given name "Ze <u>Dong</u>." So, *Wei Dong* meant to defend or to protect Chairman Mao.

Like all other Educated Youths, she was sent to a farm near N-city to be re-educated in 1968. Also, in 1970 when this factory was founded, *Wei Dong* and some other educated youths were recruited. Because she had finished her senior high school education, and was regarded as academically better educated among the Educate Youth, she was assigned to teach in the attached elementary school.

Wei Dong's parents lived in N-city, so she had the twelve-day Home Leave each year. However, instead of going to N-city to see her parents, she visited *Shao Shan*, Chairman Mao's home town. She would buy some revolutionary souvenirs there, and gave to her students.

She had a boyfriend who was her high school classmate. Since he was from the family of Red Types, he was able to join the Chinese Air Force, and to avoid being sent to the countryside or the farm. About a year after, he became a member of the Party and had the prospect to be promoted. During the reviewing process, he reported to his superior that he had *Wei Dong* as his girlfriend. After he revealed more details about her family background, the superior decided that unless the girl could join the Party, he either would be skipped for the promotion, or say good-bye to this girlfriend. As a result, *Wei Dong* desperately wanted to join the Party. Volunteer activities such as cleaning latrines, was very popular among those who wanted to join the Party. This was why she had been cleaning the public latrine every day.

Those days, when somebody was admitted as the Party member, the event would be announced in the all-hands meeting so that everybody would clap to congratulate the new Party member. But after two years, there was no such an announcement for *Wei Dong*. On the other hand, *Wei Dong's* boyfriend could not wait any longer, and married another girl from the family of the Red Types.

Depressed and disheartened, she fell ill. She got appendicitis, but was initially misdiagnosed by the doctor in our company's attached clinic. When her problem grew worse, she was transferred to the bigger and better hospital of X-city Iron and Steel Corp. She was in critical condition, with a tube inserted into her abdomen to drain the pus, developed and accumulated in the past few days. The leadership in our company sent a telegram to her parents notifying them that their daughter had been seriously ill.

There were popular songs comparing the Party as the mother that is dearer than the real mother:

"Real mother gives me the body only, but the radiance of the Party gives light to my heart," as lyrics sounded.

Now, the Party mother called on the real mother to take care of the ill daughter. Upon receiving the telegram, her mother immediately came to the hospital. They had not seen each other for years since *Wei Dong* drew the line of demarcation in 1966. Under her mother's care, she not only recovered her sick body, but also repaired her sour relationship with her parents. From then on, she started visiting her parents on her Home Leave. With help from her parents, she found a new boyfriend, with a college degree and lived in some other city. Then they married, and her husband transferred to our factory in a couple of years.

In addition to my colleagues, during my business trips, I had chances to meet many interesting people on the trains or in the hotels. In one of the trips, I met a young man who was in the same compartment of the sleeping car as mine. He was a son of the Party Secretary of N-city Diesel Engine Factory. The Party secretary was the number one leader in all organizations.

He was talkative and spoke frankly. He first talked about the "backdoor," a nickname for the way people circumvent regulations by using their connections. At that time, there was a campaign for Educated Youth: "going to the mountain area and the countryside for farming." All the high school graduates must leave the cities. But, it was the children of the ordinary citizens who didn't have connections that would have to leave. And their *Hu Kou* (residential registration) was moved out of the cities by the public security department. This meant that they did not have rationed foods and other benefits. Even they could manage to live without the rationed supplies, the police would come to interfere.

However, some high-ranking officers' children were able to avoid this. Those officers would have old comrades-in-arms[87] working in military units. What they did was call those comrades and ask them for help. Then those comrades would arrange to recruit the children of their comrades-in-arms. And once those children were recruited, they would be assigned some technical jobs so that after three years of military service, they would have the skills to work in cities, with nice paying jobs and benefits. Although at that time, there was a document from the central government to criticize this backdoor phenomenon, this document had a little effect in stopping this corruption. There was even a saying:

"If you do not use the power while you still have it, then it will expire."

It was through the "backdoor" that this young man became a driver for the provincial government. As an Educated Youth, he avoided going to the countryside by joining the PLA. He was trained in the PLA as a military truck driver. Three years later, he was dismissed, and assigned the job to drive cars. Most of the time, he drove cars and jeeps for the provincial leaders, and for high ranking officers from Beijing and other provinces.

One day, he suffered appendicitis and was admitted to a hospital. As a driver, he was not treated favorably, and was put into a big ward with a dozen patients. Although in the Marxist theory, workers were "leading class," in actuality, individual workers did not have any power or privilege. While he was there waiting and groaning, his wife decided to call her father-in-law for help.

Upon hearing the news, his father called the Party secretary of the hospital immediately. Learning this driver was no ordinary driver, but a son of a Party secretary, the hospital immediately transferred him to the operating room. The hygiene package used for him was the one normally reserved for much larger operations, such as the stomach or liver operations, and the best surgeon was called for this operation. Afterwards, he was transferred to a VIP ward reserved for high ranking officers.

"Ah! After so many years of the Cultural Revolution, people still kowtow to officers. The old habit is quite stubborn indeed!" He sighed, bitterly.

---

[87]   After the Liberation, many military officers became civilian officers.

He told me more stories about some farms in the mountain areas. There was a county where the temperature differences between the day and the night are large. This climate is very suitable to grow watermelons, and some PLA soldiers operated a watermelon farm there. They used only the traditional organic fertilizers, and pesticides were strictly forbidden. They also used a special instrument to check the sweetness in order to determine whether the watermelon was ripe. Those watermelons were not sold to the general public, but instead reserved for the central leaders in Beijing. Once this young fellow was assigned the task to transport the ripe watermelons to a military airport, and then airlift them to Beijing. It took about eight hours one way from the farm to the airport. The drivers would have the privilege to buy those watermelons at the market price, with the limit of 100 kilograms for each driver.

"I have never tasted watermelons as delicious as these ones before, nor have I tasted such watermelons after." He told me.

He also said that there were some other farms, growing tea trees, vegetables, and other fruits, for central leaders only. They were widely known as "Special Supplies."

In addition to those interesting stories, he also expressed his opinions about leadership.

"Is it difficult to be a mayor, a secretary of the province, etc.? No. If you can manage your family, then you can manage a city, a province, or even a country. The basic principles are the same. Of course, a city, a province, or a country is much larger than a family. As a head of household (in China a man was regarded as the de facto head of a family), you must do many things yourself. When you are a leading officer in the government, you would have many secretaries and assistants. You only need to assign different tasks to appropriate subordinates. In addition, for the important issues, the central government would issue documents which would give detailed instructions. You just let your assistants read and implement those instructions and check the results. When my father was appointed as the chief of the Diesel Engine Factory, he was about my age. Unfortunately, we just do not have the same kind of opportunities!" He sighed.

After the *Lin Biao*'s fall, the political atmosphere turned into a low tide. The campaign of reading Marx, Engels, and Lenin's original books did not arouse any excitement. Those books, full of political and philosophical jargons, were obscure for even those with college educations, let alone for the mass of illiterate or near illiterate citizens. In early 1974, a new political campaign started: "Criticize *Lin Biao* and Criticize Confucius," probably to recharge people's revolutionary enthusiasm. It was said that when *Lin Biao's* house was searched, many Confucius quotations were discovered in his notebooks. Therefore, Confucius was blamed to have influenced *Lin Biao*.

A caricature was created in the newspapers to represent Confucius, and was given a nickname *Kong Lao Er* (Kong the second. It was said that Confucius was the second child of his parents). A couple of people got excited and started giving speeches blaming *Kong Lao Er*, or Confucius. Even the famous writer, *Ba Jin*, published an article "Criminal Life of Confucius."[88] Those articles were too historical, theoretical, and too irrelevant to our daily life, so most people would attend the meetings as required, and recite some key words from the newspapers, but few were as enthusiastic as they were in the early stages of the Cultural Revolution. People simply thought the political campaign became games of the historians and commentators. People did not understand what made those writers so excited to blame Confucius, who lived more than 2000 years ago. Many people thought those writers going to office had nothing else do to, so they produced those things to fulfil their working obligations. To the general public, those writers seemed out of touch with the ordinary people.

However, there was a subtle hint that appeared in those articles. In addition to criticizing *Lin Biao* and Confucius, *Zhou Gong* (Duke of *Zhou*) was added. In our history class, we learned that Duke of *Zhou* was a *Zai Xiang* in the early *Zhou* Dynasty, which is from 1046 B.C. to 256 B.C. When Duke of *Zhou* died in 1105 B.C., Confucius did not yet come to this world. How would Duke *Zhou* be associated with *Lin Biao* and Confucius? These articles never even hinted at any possible connections at first. Then, gradually those articles repeatedly mentioned that Duke of *Zhou* was a *Zai Xiang*, which was equivalent to the prime minister. With the keyword "*Zhou*" and other keywords "Prime Minister" appearing together so many

---

[88]   He later regretted about the articles written during the Cultural Revolution and recommended setting up a Museum of the Cultural Revolution to prevent similar political campaign from happening in the future... But his suggestion was not adopted.

times, people came to realize the unsaid message: Premier *Zhou Enlai* could be the next target.

We were all astonished by the complexity of the power struggle at the top level. It seemed that those who became the second in the Party totem pole were doomed. *Liu Shaoqi*, the vice chairmen of the Party and the President of the PRC was the first to fall from the second position. *Lin Biao* was the next. After *Lin Biao*'s fall, Premier *Zhou* ranked next to Mao. Was it now Premier *Zhou*'s turn? We dared not to think further. From the newspapers, we knew that Premier *Zhou* was actually single-handedly running this country, busy with both domestic and international affairs. If he was to fall, who would replace him?

Unlike eight years earlier, when Chairman Mao wrote his big character poster "Bombard the Headquarters" and when the newspaper called upon people to denounce the "Khrushchev of China," young students would take the hint and rush to attack President *Liu Shaoqi*. This time, young students were no longer as frantic as their elder brothers and sisters. Having watched their brothers and sisters who were somewhat insanely loyal to Chairman Mao in 1966-1967, some even died for Mao's Revolutionary Line, and then were sent to villages, or far away board-areas, the current young students were busy trying everything they could to avoid being sent away from their homes. For example, learning singing, dancing, and playing music instruments were in vogue, because every organization had a Mao Zedong Thought propaganda team. With such skills, one would have advantages over other applicants to be recruited by factories or to join the PLA. So, the new campaign failed to arouse any interest. With the revolution having dragged on for eight long years, not only were people like a rubber band that had been stretched too much for too long and lost elasticity, but also more and more people became cynical.

In June of 1974, the newspaper reported that Premier *Zhou* was admitted to a hospital. This was a quite surprise to most people, as Premier *Zhou* had been shown a very energetic image to the public. He was famous for working long hours during the Cultural Revolution. His pictures frequently appeared in the newspaper when he was busy receiving foreign government heads and guests. Once I read a report saying when he attended a meeting in the Great Hall of the People, he was able to take two or three steps at a time climbing upstairs so that the young journalist had hard time to keep up with the Premier.

The health conditions of the top leaders were top state secret, so there was no way for us ordinary citizens to learn what disease could make the Premier be admitted to the hospital, and unprecedentedly his sickness was reported to the public. In the past, the central leaders' deceases were always revealed in their obituaries, and it was always stated in this way: they died "due to the deceases that all treatments failed," without naming the deceases in details.

At first, we were deeply concerned. But this concern was somewhat relieved after newspapers reported that Premier *Zhou* had received foreign delegations, or government heads, in the hospital. His pictures were also in the newspaper, and it appeared that he was losing weight. But, with his senior age and being in hospital, people would think this was not unusual.

Near the end of 1974, there was a big-character-poster authored by *Li Yi Zhe* and posted in *Guangzhou*, known as Canton in the West. The title of the poster was "On Socialist Democracy and Legal System." This very long poster criticized *Lin Biao*, which was what the top leaders called for at that time. It also emphasized the democracy, the rule by law, and against privileged groups. The author *Li Yi Zhe* was a pen-name of three authors. Each author has one character of their names used in this pen-name.

This poster was so popular that the readers caused traffic jams in that section of the city. People also hand-copied it and circulated nationwide. It was said that it was also circulated to Hong Kong, Taiwan, and overseas. And although the poster used many words to praise the Cultural Revolution and Chairman Mao, the *Guangdong* government soon declared that this poster was counter-revolutionary. The three authors were arrested and sentenced to long prison time.[89] After reading the hand-copied version, several my friends and I believed that the word democracy and the opposition of privileged group could be the causes of this crackdown.

In early 1973, a document from the central government was conveyed to the public that Deng Xiaoping had been appointed as a vice-premier. Deng Xiaoping had been accused as the second largest capitalist roader,

---

[89]   In 1979, after the end of the Cultural Revolution, the three were rehabilitated.

and was deprived of all his posts in 1966. But he was allowed to keep his membership in the Party. After *Lin Biao's* fall, the veteran cadres were gradually rehabilitated and returned to power again. So, Deng's coming back was not a big surprise to us.

In early 1975, there was another document from the central government. It announced some new appointments for Deng Xiaoping: he was appointed as the deputy premier minister, a vice chairman of the central military committee of the CPC, and the Chief of Staff of the PLA. This made Deng's power next to that of Chairman Mao and Premier Zhou. He was known to have demonstrated outstanding talent during the period of "Adjust, Consolidate, Substantiate, and Improve" from 1962 to 1965 after the great famine from 1959-1962.

It was not hard to tell that the nation was not in good shape after almost nine years of the political campaigns, one after the other. People's enthusiasm kept dwindling. The production in our factories was not normal. Workers were using the factory's equipment and materials to make things for themselves, for example, making the Mahjong pieces. Mahjong was regarded as a decadent game in feudal society and declared illegal after the Liberation. To make the pieces, they glued two different colored plastic plates together so that the thickness was comparable to that of the traditional Mahjong piece. Then a milling machine was used to cut the plate into blanks. Finally, one side of the piece was hand carved one by one, to make a full set of Mahjong pieces.

In addition to Mahjong sets, workers also made knives with stainless steel and hard alloys, dumbbells, reclining chairs, stoves, the mold to make honeycomb briquette, etc.

Once I went on a business trip to Shanghai and met a PLA officer[90] on the train. He was from a factory in S-province. The workers there did the same as workers in our factory. With common sense, it was not hard to figure out that this kind of activities were everywhere during those days.

Upon returning to his leadership position, Deng Xiaoping issued a directive which used Mao's words to emphasize that we must strive to

---

[90] During that time, the PLA uniforms had two types. One with only two breast pockets, which was for soldiers. The other had four pockets and was for military officers. That was the way we could tell the difference between a soldier and an officer.

improve the nation's economy. There was a short period in 1975, the economic situation seemed to improve.

However, this did not last long. In August 1975, another political campaign was launched by Chairman Mao. This time, it was criticizing a classic novel "Water Margin" (also translated as "Outlaws of the Marsh") and its hero *Song Jiang*. Mr. *Song* was labeled as a capitulator in the major newspapers. Here it came again. People were just bewildered as to why we would put such large effort into criticizing an historical novel and denouncing its fictional figure when the national economy was falling apart.

We were not literary commentators, nor would most of us be interested to become ones. The general public had tired of those political campaigns, and became totally indifferent. When rallies were organized to criticize the novel and *Song Jiang*, people would leave, one by one, shortly after the rallies started. They would go back to the dormitories and play Go, Porker, or Mahjong.

Finally, in the last quarter of the 1975, a new campaign started to aim at some real and present-day target. The most noticeable phrase that appeared in the newspapers was "the Capitalist Roader is still going (the capitalist road)." The accusations became more and more explicit, and were intensified by the invention of some new phrases, such as "that big Capitalist Roader who never regrets," "the largest diehard Capitalist Roader inside the Party," etc.

For those who went through the Cultural Revolution, it was not difficult to figure out that Deng Xiaoping was in trouble again. He was accused as the second largest Capitalist Roader in 1966. After *Liu Shaoqi*, the number one capitalist roader, died in 1969, he would naturally become the largest living Capitalist Roader inside the Party. So, he was the target of these articles.

In our attached medical clinic, there was a young man, Mr. *Guan*, who came from the farm where the majority of workers were recruited. On the farm, he had become a barefoot doctor, because his cousin was a well-known doctor of Chinese traditional medicine. Since then, he had studied a lot of books on Chinese traditional medicine as well as on modern western medicine.

Influenced by my father, I am also interested in Chinese medicine and had read some books about traditional Chinese medicine. I did not become a doctor because my elder brother, who was a physician, strongly recommended that I study engineering.

"One doctor is enough in our family," he insisted.

Due to this common interest, Dr. *Guan* and I quickly became friends. In addition to discussing Chinese medicine, we also analyzed political situations from time to time, because our life was hanging on it.

We noticed that whenever the pictures of the top-level leaders in important meetings were published, those leaders' seats were arranged in the following way: Chairman Mao would always sit at the center. Then on his right side was Premier *Zhou*, and on *Zhou's* right side were revolutionary veterans. On Mao's left side were those who rose to power during the Cultural Revolution. This seemed to hint that there were two rival factions among the top-level leaders. We called the right-side leaders as the faction of veterans, and the left side the faction of the Cultural Revolution. If they showed their separate sittings publicly while Mao was still alive, what would happen after Chairman Mao passed away?

We were deeply concerned and desperately wanted to know more about the situation at the top. Unfortunately, the task of the official media was for propaganda, so there was no way for the ordinary people to learn the truth about the situation. The "Reference News" would tell us a little more, but not the critical issues because the translated information, published by foreign media, was also filtered. Only the news and comments that were regarded favorable were translated as the supplement to the official media. Consequently, we tried hard to collect information through the grapevine.

At that time, there were indeed many rumors. One of them was this: Chairman Mao once had a meeting with Deng Xiaoping and *Wang Hongwen*, who was the vice-chairman of the CPC and later became a member of the "Gang of Four." Mao asked Mr. *Wang* first:

"What would happen after I go to see Marx?"[91]

Wang answered:

"Chinese people would continue holding Mao's flag, carrying out Mao's Cultural Revolution, and keep China in red color forever!"

Then Mao turned to Deng Xiaoping. Deng answered bluntly:

---

[91]   Many Chinese leaders used the phrase "Go to see Marx" to mean when they die.

"There would be civil wars among the warlords."

By the war lords, Deng implied the PLA generals.

There was no way for us to verify whether this conversation really took place. But the words "civil wars" had great impact on us. With the first-hand experience in the fighting between two factions and its chaotic consequences in 1967, we believed Deng's rumored assessment seemed to make more sense.

What would we do if the civil wars really were to happen? After some discussion, I thought learning acupuncture and Chinese traditional medicine could be the best answer. Our factory was surrounded by villages, and we often passed nearby villages when we went for a walk. We did not see any clinics in those villages, let alone a hospital. So, traditional medical doctors could make a living in practicing there. Also, at that time, there was no strict licensing regulations for practicing medicine in China. With barefoot doctors in vogue, I could very well be one of them. So, I started to learn acupuncture from Dr. *Guan*. I bought a set of needles and started practicing on my own legs. Also, when we went for a walk, Dr. *Guan* would teach me to recognize the various herbs grown locally, and what their medical applications would be.

On New Year's Day, two poems of Chairman Mao were published on the front pages of all newspapers. It appeared to me that the main purpose of the poems was that Chairman Mao wanted to show his fighting spirit again. However, many people also noticed the unsteady handwritten signature of Chairman Mao. This indicated that Chairman Mao's hand was shaking when writing these characters. Comparing to his early calligraphy, it was not hard for ordinary people to tell that the signature showed his very poor health conditions, even though the newspapers continued to praise Mao's excellent health as usual. Also, from the published pictures of Chairman Mao in the recent years, we could see that Chairman Mao's health deteriorated precipitously after *Lin Biao* event.

Mao Zedong thought was praised as the telescope and microscope in detecting counter-revolutionist and revisionist, etc. And he famously warned people to be vigilant about Khrushchev-like revisionists "sleeping beside us". Yet it was Chairman Mao, who hand-picked *Lin Biao* as his new top lieutenant and successor in 1966. This succession plan was even written into the Party's constitution in its Ninth Congress. So, his "telescope and microscope" failed to detect *Lin Biao*, his closest comrade-in-arms, who was accused as a traitor and the head of counter-revolutionary clique, and even developed the plot "571 Project", after only five years. This political blunder not only made the great helmsman lose face, but also badly damaged his health.

On January 8, 1976, I was awakened by official funeral music from loudspeakers which were nearly everywhere in the city. Generally, this was a signal that some central leader died. I got up and listened to the obituary to see who had died. It was Premier *Zhou*! We had hoped that he would succeed Chairman Mao to bring the country back to normal, because he was younger than Chairman Mao. Now this hope shattered. Only from the obituary, did I learn that he died of cancer.

Years later, from some commemoration articles, we learned that he was diagnosed with bladder cancer in middle of 1972. This made us realize why Deng Xiaoping was "liberated" in early 1973. At *Zhou*'s memorial service, Deng Xiaoping did the eulogy. Showing up publicly could be a good sign for Deng. We thought he might be spared this time because of his outstanding administrative talent, and his seniority in the Party.

A shocking news was broadcasted on April 8, 1976. The People's Daily published an article titled "A Counter-Revolutionary Event in Tiananmen Square." I was astonished to see such the word "counter-revolutionary" being associated with Tiananmen Square. This was unprecedented in the short PRC history. All mass events in the Square were absolutely revolutionary because the events were always organized by the government. This was the very first "counter-revolutionary event" that occurred at the center of the country's capital since the founding of the PRC.

After reading it, I learned that on Sunday, April 5, a large mass rally had occurred there, and authorities had cracked it down. In the article, a quoted counter-revolutionary poem was:

> I am in the misery of grief, but ghosts were yelling.
> I am wailing but beasts were laughing.
> A glass of wine I am holding,

As a great libation to heroes.
With my eyebrows raising,
Out of the sheath the sward I am drawing!

Through the grapevine, especially through those who had business trips to Beijing during that time, we learned more about the details.

April 4, 1976 was the *Qingming* festival, the traditional day of mourning for the dead. During that period in 1976, a huge number of wreaths were placed in Tiananmen Square around the Monument to People's Heroes, to commemorate Premier *Zhou*. However, the wreaths were removed at night. People were infuriated and held a rally on Sunday.

China has a long history of literary inquisition. People were executed for only saying something which offended the royal court. So, through the long history, people developed a very subtle and roundabout way to express their true intention while covering it with a legitimate mask. In *Zhou*'s official eulogy, he was given the title "an excellent member of the Chinese Communist Party, a great proletarian revolutionist, outstanding communist fighter, long-tested eminent leader of the Party and of the country." Under the circumstance of that time, it would be perfectly legal for people to openly commemorate Premier *Zhou*. Yet, it had been hinted that he was the intended target during the "Criticizing *Lin Biao* and Confucius" and "Criticizing Water Margin" political campaigns in the previous two years. By giving the hinted target such unprecedented love and respect, people actually indirectly expressed their frustrations with the Cultural Revolution and with *Jiang Qing* and her clique. Some people even pointed at Chairman Mao, who was mentioned in some speeches as the *Xiandai Qin Shi Huang* (modern "first emperor of Qin Dynasty").

After the commemoration event had been cracked down in Sunday evening, a nationwide search was initiated to see who was in Tiananmen Square during that period. Those who copied the poems and recorded the speeches from Tiananmen Square were required to turn those counter-revolutionary materials over to their unit leaders, or face politically criminal charges. X-city is far away from Beijing, so in our factory, people just pretended that they had not heard anything about these poems and speeches, and nobody was charged.

Soon after that, a document from the central government announced that Deng Xiaoping was that backer of this counter-revolutionary event. He was again deprived of all his power, but was allowed again to keep his membership in the Party. Mr. *Hua Guofeng* was appointed as the deputy chairman of the Party, and the prime minister. After that a new political campaign started: "Criticize Deng and Counterattack his Right Tendency of Reversing (the Cultural Revolution)."

During this new campaign, many Deng's speeches were distributed by the central committee of the Party, as reference materials for denouncing Deng. One interesting point that he made was that all employees in China had not had any raise since 1958, so it was necessary to give raises to them. By that time, most people no longer read any of those distributed "reference materials." But a few activists did read them. They'd speak during the denouncing meetings, mentioning this point, and said:

"We do not want Deng's stinky capitalist money!"

Upon hearing this, those who had not read those materials went back to find those words, and made sure that Deng had indeed said that. Gradually people started to realize that Deng Xiaoping wanted to do something good for ordinary people like us, and started to have some good feeling toward him.

On July 21, 1976, one of Chairman Mao's speech was published. Since he made this speech on July 21, 1968, it was called "7-21 Instruction." He said:

"We still need to run universities, here I mean mainly the engineering and science universities. But the length of schooling must be shortened, the education revolution must be carried out, the proletarian politics must be in the foremost place. Follow the example of Shanghai Machine Tool Factory to train the engineers from workers."

As a result, many factories launched "7-21 Worker's Universities." Our factory also started one. About 20 young workers enrolled. Two engineers and I were appointed as professors. Based on the specialty of our factory, three courses were taught: calculus, theoretical mechanics, and mechanics of materials.

In late 1975, the Chinese translation of "Mathematical Manuscripts of Karl Marx" was published. Because Karl Marx was regarded as the

Messiah of the communist movement, his manuscripts would also be authoritative. The North-West University of China adopted some calculus related materials from Marx's Manuscripts in its newly published textbook of Advanced Mathematics. This textbook was used by many universities, as well as "7-21 Worker's Universities," including ours.

July 28, 1976, a powerful magnitude-7.8 earthquake hit *Tangshan,* a big industrial city about 140 miles northeast of Beijing. This was the largest and the most damaging earthquake ever heard of by my generation.

After that, newspapers reported many unusual signs that had occurred before this devastating earthquake. One such a report hailed an engineer as a hero, as he had stopped his passenger train when he saw some unusually strong white light in the sky just before the earthquake, shortly after the train left the *Tangshan* Railroad Station. This avoided a potentially catastrophic accident.

There were other reports about unusual activities of birds, animals, and fish before this earthquake. From then on, the whole country was in earthquake panic. If somebody noticed some birds or animal activities they thought were unusual, or if somebody noticed strange shaped clouds, some unusual sounds, etc., earthquake warnings would be issued. People would sleep in tents for days to avoid any possible disasters like the one in *Tangshan.*

Sept. 9, 1976, I was chatting with Dr. *Guan* in his room after the noon nap, and somebody knocked on the door and notified us that there was an important news broadcast scheduled at 4:00 p.m. This made us nervous because this was unprecedented. By then, all important news broadcasts had been always scheduled at 8:00 p.m. in the Central Radio Station's "*Xin wen Lian Bo*" (Anchored News Broadcast) program. What could cause this important news broadcast to be announced so urgently so that it would occur four hours before the regular time? We guessed that there could be two likely events. One was that Chairman Mao might have passed away. Another was that the Soviet Unit might have launched a nuclear attack on us.

We turned on our radio set and waiting. At 4:00 p.m. sharp, the official funeral music was played. This confirmed that our first guess was correct. We noticed that this report was not called an "obituary", but the "Announcement to entire Party, entire Army, and all people of the country." In addition, in the previous obituaries for central leaders, announcements would state the date and time of the death, and then report their ages. But the age was not mentioned in Chairman Mao's obituary.

An interesting thing about 1976 was that on March 8, 1976, there was a meteorite shower in *Jilin* province. The largest of these meteorites was nearly 4000 pounds, producing a crater of about 7 ft. in diameter and 21 ft. in depth, and causing a shake equivalent to a magnitude-1.7 earthquake.

In many classical novels, there are descriptions that when a star falls from the sky, some important person would die soon. After Chairman Mao passed away, people started to talk about the meteorite shower in March, and the earthquake in July. A lot of Chinese genuinely believed that the two phenomena were the omens predicting Chairman Mao's death. There were rumors that the meteorite shower, and especially the earthquake, disturbed Chairman Mao himself as well. After Marshal *Zhu De* died on July 6, 1976, he said to his assistants that he would be the next.

The memorial service for Chairman Mao was held on September 18, 1976, in Tiananmen Square. But our gut feeling told us that this was not the end of the story yet.

Officially, the Deputy Chairman of CPC, *Hua Guofeng*, became the highest leader in China after Mao's death. However, he was 55 years old in 1976. There were a lot of revolutionary veterans whose ranks and seniority were higher or much higher than Mr. *Hua* when the PRC was founded. Historically in China, seniority has been a very important asset in the political arena. Could *Hua Guofeng* really continue to hold power? Would those marshals and generals obey him? Would Mao's wife and her followers obey him? Many of my friends and I were anxious.

We carefully examined the published pictures since the time of Mao's death, checked the expressions of the leaders one by one, especially how the two rival cliques looked at each other. We tried hard to decipher clues for the future from those subtle signs. But this digging proved to be extremely difficult, as they all looked sullen and emotionless in the pictures, pretty much like statues. Then, gradually, the newspapers started to give some clues.

After Chairman Mao's death, there was an alleged Supreme Directive: "Act according to the established principles."

We thought this might be Mao's last words, advising the new leaders to continue Chairman Mao's policies. So, everything would remain the same as during the past 10 years. But after a while, this "Supreme Directive" was no longer mentioned in the official media. Instead, editorials and remarks started to suggest that somebody had "faked and tampered with" Chairman Mao's Supreme Directives. This gave the signal that perhaps Mao might not have said "Act according to the established principles." So, the situation became more complicated.

Through the grapevine, we learned that the Shanghai militia had nine divisions with three million militiamen, and was equipped with modern military gear, comparable to that of the PLA. And we knew that Shanghai was the base of the Cultural Revolution clique. This news seemed to indicate that civil war was imminent. We were all worried.

On October 18, 1976, a document issued from the central leadership announced that Mao's wife *Jiang Qing, Zhang Chunqiao, Yao Wenyuan,* and *Wang Hongwen* were named as the "Gang of Four." They were deprived of all their positions and were arrested. This marked the official end of the Cultural Revolution, and a catastrophic civil war was avoided. The people all over the country were so happy to celebrate that all wines and liquors were sold out in all stores in China on that day because of this grass-root celebration. Chairman Mao's era had finally come to the end.

Epilog

Although Mao's era had ended, but his legacy had not. Soon after the fall of the Gang of Four, the central government decided to build a memorial hall on the south side of Tiananmen Square.

In addition, there were many wide-spread rumors about Chairman Mao. For example, why the garrison of the central guards was called 8341 in Mao's era? It was said that Chairman Mao once visited a Daoist monk and the monk predicted that he would be in power for 41 years and die at the age of 83. Most people know that Mao became the most powerful leader in 1935 during the long march. By 1976, he had indeed been in power for 41 years. And he was born in 1893, so he was 83-years-old in 1976. Although when he died, it was more than three months short of his 83rd birthday, in old Chinese custom a person would be immediately one year old upon birth. Therefore, he was 83 in 1976. Some official articles were published to discredit this rumor. Nevertheless, a lot of people still repeatedly tell this story during their chit chats, even in the present days.

On the Internet, there is another interesting story about the statue of Chairman Mao.

A Chairman Mao's statue was manufactured in *Nanjing*. This was built for *Shaoshan*, Mao's hometown. The statue is six meters high with a 4.1-meter base, which implies that he was in power for 41 years. The total height is 10.1 Meter, meaning October 1, the day the PRC was founded, and implying he was the founding father of the PRC.

On Dec. 2, 1993, the workers tried to lift the statue onto a truck. But no matter what efforts were made, the crane could not lift it. Then some people discovered that the rope had been tied in the wrong place: it was around the neck of Chairman Mao! After people moved the rope to the bottom of the base, the statue was easily lifted and put into place. Then the truck left for *Shaoshan*.

It was originally planned for the truck to arrive in *Changsha*, the capital city of *Hunan* province, in the evening. However, when the truck was in *Jiangxi* province and near the border between *Jiangxi and Hunan*, the truck stalled. The driver could not restart the engine, nor could he find anything wrong. So, the driver decided to stay in *Jiangxi* for that night. Local people told the driver that the location was close to the red base *Jinggang* Mountain, which was established in 1927 by Mao. The engine stalled because Chairman Mao must have been reminiscent of the red base, and wanted to stay here longer. Next day, the driver said to the statue:

"Chairman, let's go now."

Then, miraculously, he was able to start the engine without any issue. When the status arrived at *Shaoshan*, local people had been waiting there and the crowd along the road stretched several miles. When the truck appeared, people shouted excitedly:

"Chairman Mao returned home!"

Moreover, on that day, the sun and the moon appeared at the same time, a phenomenon regarded as very propitious.

Nowadays, it is not uncommon for drivers, especially taxi drivers, to hang small Chairman Mao's portraits in their automobiles, in the hope that Chairman Mao would protect them from accidents.

On the other hand, in 1979, a shocking story about Ms. *Zhang Zhixin* was published in the People's Daily. Her crime was criticizing Chairman Mao, and was condemned to death as an "active counter-revolutionist." Before her execution, her throat was cut to prevent her from speaking or shouting. This inhuman treatment was astonishing because when communist party members, such as Mr. *Qu Qiubai*, were executed by KMT, they were allowed to shout communist slogans and singing revolutionary songs. Now, her right to speak the last words was deprived. Although she had been rehabilitated in 1978 after the Cultural Revolution, her remains were not yet found even to date.

After the fall of the Gang of four, Mr. *Chen* and his family applied to go back to Hong Kong. In early 1977, their application was approved.

The family of four moved to their hometown after a quarter of a century. We were sorry to see them leave. In the meantime, we were also glad to see their reunion with their families and relatives in Hong Kong. By leaving all the painful memory behind, they would turn a new leaf in their lives, especially the new leaves of their children's lives.

When they were leaving, the universities were still enrolling the worker-peasant-soldier students based on recommendation by their units, rather than by entrance examination. And there were almost no chances of the children from the problematic family background to be recommended to attend colleges. But with their good grades, they would certainly be able to attend colleges in Hong Kong.

Since our factory was close to the railroad, we frequently saw slogans painted on the trains, such as "Salute Deng Xiaoping who had fearlessly fought with the Gang of Four!" Then the movie "*Jia Wu Feng Yun*" which was a historical drama about the naval battle in 1894 with Japan. General *Deng Shichang* was the hero in the movie. In the movie, there was a scene showing people called:

"Sir *Deng,* please lead us fighting Japanese troop."

Due to the same surname Deng, it appeared to us that this was a subtle signal hinting that Deng Xiaoping would be back into power again. And sure enough, soon he was "liberated." One of the important things Deng Xiaoping did was to restore the entrance examinations for the college and the graduate programs.

In 1978, I passed two rounds of examinations to become one of the first batch of graduate students after the Cultural Revolution. Upon graduation, I was assigned to teach in W-city Institute of Iron and Steel.

According to the historical reality my father was wrongly charged. As mentioned earlier, when my father worked as a county mayor, the KMT and the CPC were in the united front. Both parties were partners, not enemies. Also, according to the Party and the government's policy, my father made a contribution to the peaceful liberation of the Alexa area, so, he was promised that he would never be charged in the future. However, fearing that we would be charged as not drawing a clear demarcation with our "counter-revolutionary father", we never dared to appeal.

In 1979, after learning that the central government issued a document to review the incorrect charge of the rightists, we finally summoned the courage to appeal. We wrote a letter describing all those historical facts, and asked our uncle, who was rehabilitated as the people's representative, to hand it directly to Mr. *Xi Zhongxun*, who was the political commissar when negotiation of the peaceful liberation of Alxa and also liberated from his own political trouble after the Cultural Revolution, during a meeting of the National People's Congress. One year later, our appeal was granted and my father was rehabilitated. We were also given 500 Yuan as the compensation. Although this was less than 5 months of my father's monthly salary, politically this rehabilitation was significant. Based on the past experience, we were relieved that our offspring would never have to suffer what our generation had suffered. We all gladly celebrated it.

In 1984, after passing the examination, I was selected to study abroad. In February 1985, the new rules for studying abroad were issued. Previous rules had limits that for those who were more than 40, and those who had a Master's degree and higher, were not allowed to pursue studies leading to higher degrees. New rules no longer had those limits.

According to the new rules, as long as one could obtain financial aid from a university, they could pursue their further studies, which led to higher degrees. I immediately started to contact the universities. Dr. Stephen L. Rice, the head of Mechanical Engineering and Aerospace Sciences at the University of Central Florida, contacted me for an interview at the Westin Bay Shore Hotel, where he was attending a technical conference. After that, the University of Central Florida accepted me with the condition that I must take the TOEFL and GRE exams in my first semester. Also, the department of Mechanical Engineering and Aerospace Sciences agreed to give me an assistantship to financing my study. Dr. Rice was my advisor, with my dissertation on the computer-aided conceptual design.

After my graduation with a PhD degree in the summer of 1989, a local company "Control Automation" offered me a position as a software engineer to develop CAD/CAM software. Recalling Dan Rather of CBS reported, in real time, what had happened in Tiananmen Square, I accepted the offer. Control Automation sponsored my H1 working visa application. After that I was able to apply for the green card, and eventually become an American citizen in 1999. My wife and daughter joined me in 1987, and also became American citizens in 1999.

Printed in the United States
By Bookmasters